I0093633

Ouida

# Two little wooden shoes

A sketch

Ouida

**Two little wooden shoes**
*A sketch*

ISBN/EAN: 9783742835949

Manufactured in Europe, USA, Canada, Australia, Japa

Cover: Foto ©Thomas Meinert / pixelio.de

Manufactured and distributed by brebook publishing software
(www.brebook.com)

Ouida

**Two little wooden shoes**

# COLLECTION

## OF

# BRITISH AUTHORS

## TAUCHNITZ EDITION.

### VOL. 1387.

TWO LITTLE WOODEN SHOES BY OUIDA.

IN ONE VOLUME.

# TAUCHNITZ EDITION.

## By the same Author,

# TWO LITTLE
# WOODEN SHOES.

## A SKETCH.

BY

## OUIDA,

**AUTHOR OF**
"IDALIA," "A DOG OF FLANDERS," "PASCARÈL," ETC.

*COPYRIGHT EDITION.*

## LEIPZIG
## BERNHARD TAUCHNITZ
### 1874.

*The Right of Translation is reserved.*

# TWO LITTLE WOODEN SHOES.

## A SKETCH.

---

### CHAPTER I.

BÉBÉE sprang out of bed at daybreak. She was sixteen.

It seemed a very wonderful thing to be as much as that—sixteen—a woman quite.

A cock was crowing under her lattice—he said how old you are!—how old you are! every time that he sounded his clarion.

She opened the lattice and wished him good-day, with a laugh. It was so pleasant to be woke by him and to think that no one in all the world could ever call her a child any more.

There was a kid bleating in the shed. There was a thrush singing in the dusk of the sycamore leaves. There was a calf lowing to its mother away there beyond the fence. There were dreamy

muffled bells ringing in the distance from many
steeples and belfries where the city was; they all
said one thing: "How good it is to be so old as
that—how good, how very good!"

Bébée was very pretty.

No one in all Brabant ever denied that. To
look at her it seemed as if she had so lived amongst
the flowers that she had grown like them, and only
looked a bigger blossom—that was all.

She wore two little wooden shoes and a little
cotton cap, and a grey kirtle—linen in summer,
serge in winter; but the little feet in the shoes were
like rose-leaves, and the cap was as white as a
lily, and the grey kirtle was like the bark of the
bough that the apple blossom parts when it peeps
out to blush in the sun.

The flowers had been the only godmothers that
she had ever had, and fairy godmothers too. The
marigolds and the sunflowers had given her their
ripe rich gold to tint her hair; the lupins had lent
their azure for her eyes; the moss-rose buds had
made her pretty mouth; the arum lilies had un-
curled their softness for her skin; and the lime-

blossoms had given her their frank, fresh, innocent fragrance. The winds had blown, and the rains had rained, and the sun had shone on her, indeed, but they had only warmed the whiteness of her limbs, and had given to her body and her soul a hardy, breeze-blown freshness like that of a field cowslip.

She had never been called anything but Bébée.

One summer day Antoine Maes,—a French subject, but a Belgian by adoption and habit, an old man who got his meagre living by tilling the garden plot about his hut and selling flowers in the city squares—Antoine, going into Brussels for his day's trade, had seen a grey bundle floating amongst the water-lilies in the bit of water near his hut and had hooked it out to land, and found a year-old child in it, left to drown no doubt, but saved by the lilies, and laughing gleefully at fate.

Some lace-worker, blind with the pain of toil, or some peasant woman harder of heart than the oxen in her yoke, had left it there to drift away to death, not reckoning for the inward ripple of the current or the toughness of the lily leaves and stems.

Old Antoine took it to his wife, and the wife, a childless aged soul, begged leave to keep it; and the two poor lonely simple folks grew to care for the homeless and motherless thing, and they and the people about all called it Bébée—only Bébée.

The church got at it and added to it a saint's name; but for all its little world it remained Bébée—Bébée when it trotted no higher than the red carnation-heads;—Bébée when its yellow curls touched as high as the lavender bush;—Bébée on this proud day when the thrush's song and the cock's crow found her sixteen years old.

Old Antoine's hut stood in a little patch of garden ground with a briar hedge all round it, in that byeway which lies between Laeken and Brussels, in the heart of flat green Brabant, where there are beautiful meadows and tall flowering hedges, and forest trees, and fern-filled ditches, and a little piece of water, deep and cool, where the swans sail all day long, and the silvery willows dip and sway with the wind.

Turn aside from the highway, and there it lies

to-day; and all the place brims over with grass, and boughs, and blossoms, and flowering beans and wild dog-roses; and there are a few cottages and cabins there near the pretty water, and farther there is an old church sacred to S. Guido; and beyond goes the green, level country and the endless wheat-fields, and the old mills with their red sails against the sun; and beyond all these the pale, blue, sea-like horizon of the plains of Flanders.

It was a pretty little hut, pink all over like a sea shell, in the fashion that the Netherlanders love; and its two square lattices were dark with creeping plants and big rose-bushes; and its roof, so low that you could touch it, was golden and green with all the lichens and stoneworts that are known on earth.

Here Bébée grew from year to year; and soon learned to be big enough and hardy enough to tie up bunches of stocks and pinks for the market, and then to carry a basket for herself, trotting by Antoine's side along the green roadway and into the white, wide streets; and in the market the buyers—most often of all when they were young mothers—would seek out the little golden head and the beautiful frank blue eyes, and buy Bébée's lilies and carnations whether they wanted them or not. So that old Antoine Maes used to cross himself and say that, thanks to Our Lady, trade was thrice as stirring since the little one had stretched out her rosy fingers with the flowers.

All the same, however stirring trade might be in summer, when the long winters came and the Montagne de la Cour was a sharp slope of ice, and the pinnacles of Ste. Gudule were all frosted white with snow, and the hothouse flowers alone could fill the market, and the country gardens were bitter black wind-swept desolations where the chilly roots huddled themselves together underground like homeless children in a cellar,—then the money gained in the time of leaf and blossom was all needed to buy a black loaf and a faggot of wood; and many a day in the little pink hut Bébée rolled herself up in her bed like a dormouse, to forget in sleep that she was supperless and as cold as a frozen robin.

So that when Antoine Maes grew sick and died,

more from age and weakness than any real disease, there were only a few silver crowns in the brown jug hidden in the thatch, and the hut itself, with its patch of ground, was all that he could leave to Bébée.

"Live in it, little one, and take nobody in it to worry you, and be good to the bird and the goat, and be sure to keep the flowers blowing," said the old man with his last breath; and, sobbing her heart out by his bedside, Bébée vowed to do his bidding.

She was not quite fourteen then; and when she had laid her old friend to rest in the rough green graveyard about S. Guido, she was very sorrowful and lonely—poor little, bright Bébée, who had never hardly known a worse woe than to run the thorns of the roses into her fingers or to cry because a thrush was found starved to death in the snow.

Bébée went home, and sat down in a corner and thought.

The hut was her own, and her own the little green triangle just then crowded with its May-day

blossom in all the colours of the rainbow. She was
to live in it, and never let the flowers die—so he
had said; good, rough old ugly Antoine Maes, who
had been to her as father, mother, country, king,
and law.

The sun was shining. Through the little square
of the lattice she could see the great tulips opening
in the grass and a bough of the apple-tree swaying
in the wind. A chaffinch clung to the bough, and
swung to and fro singing. The door stood open,
with the broad bright day shining through; and
Bébée's little world came streaming in with it—the
world which dwelt in the half dozen cottages
that fringed this green lane of hers like beavers'
nests pushed out under the leaves on to the water's
edge.

They came in, six or eight of them, all women;
trim, clean, plain Brabant peasants, hard working,
kindly of nature, and shrewd in their own simple
matters; people who laboured in the fields all the
day long or worked themselves blind over the lace
pillows in the city.

"You are too young to live alone, Bébée," said

the first of them. "My old mother shall come and keep house for you."

"Nay—better come and live with me, Bébée," said the second. "I will give you bit and drop, and clothing, too, for the right to your plot of ground."

"That is to cheat her," said the third. "Hark here, Bébée—my sister, who is a lone woman, as you know well, shall come and bide with you, and ask you nothing—nothing at all—only you shall just give her a crust, perhaps, and a few flowers to sell sometimes."

"No, no," said a fourth; "that will not do. You let me have the garden and the hut, Bébée, and my sons shall till the place for you—and I will live with you myself, and leave the boys the cabin—so you will have all the gain, do you not see, dear little one?"

"Pooh!" said the fifth, stouter and better clothed than the rest. "You are all eager for your own good, not for hers. Now I—Father Francis says we should all do as we would be done by—I will take Bébée to live with me, all for nothing; and we will

root the flowers up and plant it with good cabbages
and potatoes and salad plants.   And I will stable
my cows in the hut to sweeten it after a dead man,
and I will take my chance of making money out of
it, and no one can speak more fair than that when
one sees what weather is, and thinks what insects
do; and all the year round, winter and summer,
Bébée here will want for nothing, and have to take
no care for herself whatever."

The speaker, Trine Krebs, was the best-to-do
woman in the little lane, having two cows of her
own and earrings of solid silver, and a green cart,
and a big dog that took the milk into Brussels.
She was heard, therefore, with respect, and a short
silence followed her words.   But it was very short;
and a hubbub of voices crossed each other after it
as the speakers grew hotter against one another and
more eager to convince each other of the disinter-
estedness and delicacy of their offers of aid.

Through it all Bébée sat quite quiet on the edge
of the little truckle bed, with her eyes fixed on the
apple bough and the singing chaffinch.

She heard them all patiently.

They were all her good friends, friends old and
true. This one had given her cherries a dozen of
summers. That other had bought her a little waxen
Jesus at Kermesse. The old woman in the blue
linen skirt had taken her to her first communion.
She who wanted her sister to have the crust and
the flowers, had brought her a beautiful painted
book of Hours that had cost her a whole franc.
Another had given her the solitary wonder, travel
and foreign feast of her whole life, a day fifteen
miles away at the fair at Mechlin. The last speaker
of all had danced her on her knee a hundred
times in babyhood and told her legends, and let
her ride in the green cart behind big curly-coated
Tambour.

Bébée did not doubt that these trusty old friends
meant well by her, and yet a certain heavy sense
fell on her that in all these counsels there was not
the same whole-hearted and frank goodness that
had prompted the gifts to her of the waxen Jesus,
and the book of Hours.

Bébée did not reason, because she was too little
a thing and too trustful; but she felt in a vague,

sorrowful fashion, that they were all of them trying to make some benefit out of her poor heritage, with small regard for herself at the root of their speculations.

Bébée was a child; wholly a child; body and soul were both as fresh in her as a golden crocus just born out of the snows. But she was not a little fool, though people sometimes called her so because she would sit in the moments of her leisure with her blue eyes on the far away clouds like a thing in a dream.

She heard them patiently till the cackle of shrill voices had exhausted itself, and the six women stood on the sunny mud floor of the hut eyeing each other with venomous glances; for though they were good neighbours at all times, each, in this matter, was hungry for the advantages to be got out of old Antoine's plot of ground.

They were very poor; they toiled in the scorched or frozen fields all weathers, or spent from dawn to nightfall pouring over their cobweb lace; and to save a sou or gain a cabbage was of moment to them, only second to the keeping of their souls secure of heaven by Lenten mass and Easter psalm.

Bébée listened to them all, and the tears dried on her cheeks, and her pretty rosebud lips curled close in one another.

"You are very good, no doubt, all of you," she said at last. "But I cannot tell you that I am thankful, for my heart is like a stone, and I think it is not so very much for me as it is for the hut that you are speaking. Perhaps it is wrong in me to say so—yes—I am wrong, I am sure,—you are all kind, and I am only Bébée. But you see he told me to live here and take care of the flowers, and I must do it, that is certain. I will ask Father Francis, if you wish; but if he tell me I am wrong as you do, I shall stay here all the same."

And in answer to their expostulations and condemnation, she only said the same thing over again always, in different words, but to the same steadfast purpose. The women clamoured about her for an hour in reproach and rebuke; she was a baby indeed, she was a little fool, she was a naughty, obstinate child, she was an ungrateful, wilful little creature, who ought to be beaten till she was blue, if only there was anybody that had the right to do it!

"But there is nobody that has the right," said Bébée, getting angry and standing upright on the floor, with Antoine's old grey cat in her round arms. "He told me to stay here, and he would not have said so if it had been wrong; and I am old enough to do for myself, and I am not afraid, and who is there that would hurt me? Oh, yes; go and tell Father Francis, if you like. I do not believe he will blame me, but if he do, I must bear it. Even if he shut the church door on me, I will obey Antoine, and the flowers will know I am right, and they will let no evil spirits touch me, for the flowers are strong for that; they talk to the angels in the night."

What use was it to argue with a little idiot like this? Indeed, peasants never do argue; they use abuse. It is their only form of logic.

They used it to Bébée, rating her soundly, as became people who were old enough to be her grandmothers, and who knew that she had been raked out of their own pond, and had no more real place in creation than a water-rat, as one might say.

The women were kindly, and had never thrown this truth against her before; and in fact, to be a foundling was no sort of disgrace to their sight; but anger is like wine, and makes the depths of the mind shine clear, and all the mud that is in the depths stink in the light; and in their wrath at not sharing Antoine's legacy, the good souls said bitter things that in calm moments they would no more have uttered than they would have taken up a knife to slit her throat.

They talked themselves hoarse with impatience and chagrin, and went backwards over the threshold, their wooden shoes and their shrill voices keeping a clattering chorus.

By this time it was evening; the sun had gone off the floor, and the bird had done singing.

Bébée stood in the same place, hardening her little heart, whilst big and bitter tears swelled into her eyes, and fell on the soft fur of the sleeping cat.

2*

She only very vaguely understood why it was in any sense shameful to have been raked out of the water-lilies like a drowning field-mouse, as they had said it was. She and Antoine had often talked of that summer morning when he had found her there amongst the leaves, and Bébée and he had laughed over it gaily, and she had been quite proud in her innocent fashion that she had had a fairy and the flowers for her mother and god-mothers, which Antoine always told her was the case beyond any manner of doubt.

Even Father Francis hearing the pretty harmless fiction had never deemed it his duty to disturb her pleasure in it, being a good, cheerful old man, who thought that woe and wisdom both come soon enough to bow young shoulders and to silver young curls without his interference.

Bébée had always thought it quite a fine thing to have been born of water-lilies with the sun for her father, and when people in Brussels had asked her of her parentage, seeing her stand in the market with a certain look on her that was not like other children, she had always gravely answered in the purest good faith,—

"My mother was a flower."

"You are a flower, at any rate," they would say in return, and Bébée had been always quite content.

But now she was doubtful; she was rather perplexed than sorrowful. These good friends of hers seemed to see some new sin about her. Perhaps, after all, thought Bébée, it might have been better to have had a human mother who would have taken care of her now old Antoine was dead, instead of those beautiful gleaming cold water-lilies which went to sleep on their green velvet beds, and did not certainly care when the thorns ran into her fingers, or the pebbles got in her wooden shoes.

In some vague way, disgrace and envy—the twin Discords of the world—touched her innocent cheek with their hot breath, and as the evening fell, Bébée felt very lonely and a little wistful.

She had been always used to run out in the pleasant twilight time amongst the flowers, and water them, Antoine filling the can from the well, and the neighbours would come and lean against the little low wall, knitting and gossiping; and the big dogs, released from harness, would poke their heads through the wicket for a crust; and the children would dance and play Colin Maillard on the green by the water, and she, when the flowers were no longer thirsty, would join them, and romp and dance and sing the gayest of them all.

But now the buckets hung at the bottom of the well, and the flowers hungered in vain, and the neighbours held aloof, and she shut-to the hut door and listened to the rain which began to fall, and cried herself to sleep all alone in her tiny kingdom.

When the dawn came the sun rose red and warm; the grass and boughs sparkled; a lark sang; Bébée awoke, sad in heart indeed, for her lost old friend, but brighter and braver.

"Each of them wanted to get something out of me," thought the child. "Well, I will live alone, then, and do my duty, just as he said. The flowers will never let any real harm come, though they do look so indifferent and smiling sometimes, and though not one of them hung their heads when his coffin was carried through them yesterday."

That want of sympathy in the flowers troubled her. The old man had loved them so well, and they had all looked as glad as ever, and had blossomed saucily in the sun, and not even a rosebud turned the paler as the poor still stiffened limbs went by in the wooden shell.

"I suppose God cares—but I wish they did," said Bébée, to whom the garden was more intelligible than Providence.

"Why do you not care?" she asked the pinks, shaking the raindrops off their curled rosy petals. The pinks leaned lazily against their sticks, and seemed to say, "Why should we care for anything, unless a slug be eating us?—*that* is real woe, if you like."

Bébée, without her sabots on, wandered thoughtfully among the sweet wet sun-lightened labyrinths of blossom, her pretty bare feet treading the narrow grassy paths with pleasure in their coolness.

"He was so good to you," she said reproachfully to the great gaudy gillyflowers and the painted

sweet peas. "He never let you know heat or cold
—he never let the worm gnaw or the snail harm
you;—he would get up in the dark to see after
your wants,—and when the ice froze over you, he
was there to loosen your chains. Why do you not
care, any one of you?"

"How silly you are!" said the flowers. "You
must be a butterfly or a poet, Bébée, to be as foolish
as that. Some one will do all he did. We are of
market value, you know. Care, indeed!—when the
sun is so warm, and there is not an earwig in the
place to trouble us."

The flowers were not always so selfish as this;
and perhaps the sorrow in Bébée's heart made their
callousness seem harder than it really was. When
we suffer very much ourselves, anything that smiles
in the sun seems cruel—a child, a bird, a dragonfly
—nay, even a fluttering ribbon, or a spear-grass that
waves in the wind.

There was a little shrine at the corner of the
garden, set into the wall; a niche with a bit of glass
and a picture of the Virgin, so battered that no
one could trace any feature of it. It had been there

for centuries, and was held in great veneration; and old Antoine had always cut the choicest buds of his roses and set them in a delf pot in front of it every other morning all the summer long.

Bébée, whose religion was the sweetest and vaguest mingling of Pagan and Christian myths, and whose faith in fairies and in saints was exactly equal in strength and in ignorance—Bébée filled the delf pot anew carefully, then knelt down on the turf in that little green corner, and prayed in devout hopeful childish good faith to the awful unknown Powers who were to her only as gentle guides and kindly playmates.

Was she too familiar with the Holy Mother?

She was almost fearful that she was; but then the Holy Mother loved flowers so well, Bébée could not feel aloof from her, nor be afraid.

"When one cuts the best blossoms for her, and tries to be good, and never tells a lie," thought Bébée, "I am quite sure, as she loves the lilies, that she will never altogether forget me."

So she said to the Mother of Christ fearlessly, and nothing doubting; and then rose for her

daily work of cutting the flowers for the market in
Brussels.

By the time her baskets were full, her fowls
fed, her goat foddered, her starling's cage cleaned,
and her hut door locked, and her wooden shoes
clattering on the sunny road into the city, Bébée
was almost content again, though ever and again as
she trod the familiar ways, the tears dimmed her
eyes as she remembered that old Antoine would
never again hobble over the stones beside her.

"You are a little wilful one, and too young to
live alone," said Father Francis, meeting her in
the lane.

But he did not scold her seriously; and she
kept to her resolve; and the women who were good
at heart took her back into favour again; and so
Bébée had her own way, and the fairies, or the
saints, or both together, took care of her; and so it
came to pass that all alone she heard the cock crow
whilst it was dark, and woke to the grand and
amazing truth that this fragrant dusky June morning
found her full sixteen years old.

## CHAPTER II.

THE two years had not been all playtime, any more than they had been all summer.

When one has not father, or mother, or brother, and all one's friends have barely bread enough for themselves, life cannot be very easy, nor its crusts very many at any time.

Bébée had a cherub's mouth, and a dreamer's eyes, and a poet's thoughts sometimes in her own untaught and unconscious fashion. But all the same she was a little hardworking Brabant peasant girl; up whilst the birds twittered in the dark; to bed when the red sun sank beyond the far blue line of the plains; she hoed, and dug, and watered, and planted her little plot; she kept her cabin as clean as a fresh blossomed primrose; she milked her goat, and swept her floor; she sat, all the warm days, in the town, selling her flowers, and in the winter-time, when her garden yielded her nothing,

she strained her sight over lace-making in the city
to get the small bit of food that stood between
her and that hunger which to the poor means death.

A hard life: very hard when hail and snow
made the streets of Brussels like slopes of ice; a
little hard even in the gay summer-time when Bébée
sat under the awning fronting the Maison du Roi;
but all the time the child throve on it, and was
happy, and dreamed of many graceful and gracious
things whilst she was weeding amongst her lilies,
or tracing the threads to and fro on her lace pillow.

She could not move amongst her flowers idly as
poets and girls love to do; she had to be active
amidst them, else drought and rain, and worm and
snail, and blight and brute would have made havoc
of their fairest hopes.

The loveliest love is that which dreams high
above all storms, unsoiled by all burdens; but, perhaps, the strongest love is that which, whilst it adores,
drags its feet through mire, and burns its brow in
heat for the thing beloved. So Bébée dreamed in
her garden; but all the time for sake of it hoed and
dug, and hurt her hands, and tired her limbs, and

bowed her shoulders under the great metal pails from the well.

Now—when she woke to the full sense of her wonderful sixteen years,—Bébée, standing barefoot on the mud-floor, was as pretty a sight as was to be seen betwixt Scheldt and Rhine. The sun had only left a soft warmth like an apricot's on her white skin. Her limbs, though strong as a mountain pony's, were slender and well shaped. Her hair curled in shiny crumpled masses, and tumbled about her shoulders. Her pretty round plump little breast was white as the daisies in the grass without, and in this blossoming time of her little life Bébée, in her way, was beautiful as a peach-bloom is beautiful, and her innocent, courageous, happy eyes had dreams in them underneath their laughter—dreams that went farther than the green woods of Laeken, farther even than the white clouds of summer.

She was sixteen!—quite a woman!—was it possible, she said to herself, as she went out to sit on her little wooden stool in the doorway. There had been fresh rain in the night, the garden was radiant; the smell of the wet earth was sweeter than all

perfumes that are burned in palaces. The dripping
rosebuds nodded against her hair as she went out;
the starling called to her—"Bébée, Bébée—bonjour,
bonjour," which were all the words it knew.

It said the same words a thousand times a week.
But to Bébée it seemed that the starling must
certainly be aware that she was sixteen years old
that day.

Breaking her bread into the milk she sat in the
dawn and thought, without knowing that she thought
it, "How good it is to live when one is young!"

Old people say the same thing often, but they
sigh when they say it. Bébée smiled.

Mère Kré opened her door in the next cottage
and nodded over the wall.

"What a fine thing to be sixteen!—a merry
year, Bébée."

Marthe, the carpenter's wife, came out from her
gate, broom in hand.

"The Holy Saints keep you, Bébée; why you
are quite a woman now!"

The little children of Varnhart, the charcoal-
burner, who were as poor as any mouse in the old

churches, rushed out of their little home up the lane, bringing with them a cake stuck full of sugar and seeds and tied round with a blue ribbon, that their mother had made that very week, all in her honour.

"Only see, Bébée! Such a grand cake!" they shouted, dancing down the lane; "Jules picked the plums, and Jeanne washed the almonds, and Christine took the ribbon off her own Communion cap—all for you—all for you—but you will let us come and eat it too!"

Old gran'mère Bishot, who was the oldest woman about Laeken, hobbled through the grass on her crutches and nodded her white shaking head, and smiled at Bébée.

"I have nothing to give you, little one—except my blessing, if you care for that."

Bébée ran out, breaking from the children, and knelt down in the wet grass and bent her sunny head to the benediction.

Trine Krebs, the miller's wife, the richest woman of them all, called to the child from the steps of the mill,

"A merry year and the blessing of heaven,
Bébée. Come up, and here is my first dish of
cherries for you; not tasted one myself; they will
make you a feast with Vannhart's cake, though she
should have known better, so poor as she is. Charity
begins at home, and these children's stomachs are
empty."

Bébée ran up and then down again gleefully with
her lapful of big black cherries; Tambour, the old
white dog, who had used to drag her about in his
milk-cart, leaping on her in sympathy and con-
gratulation.

"What a supper we will have!" she cried to the
charcoal-burner's children, who were turning summer-
saults in the dock-leaves, while the swans stared and
hissed.

When one is sixteen, cherries and a cake have
a flavour of Paradise still, especially when they are
tasted twice, or thrice at most, in all the year.

An old man called to her as she went by his
door.

All these little cabins lie close together, with
only their apple trees, or their tall beans, or their

hedges of thorn between them; you may ride by and never notice them if you do not look for them under the leaves closely, as you would for thrushes' nests.

He, too, was very old; a life-long neighbour and gossip of Antoine's; he had been a day-labourer in these same fields all his years, and had never travelled further than where the red mill-sails turned amongst the colza and the corn.

"Come in, my pretty one, for a second," he whispered, with an air of mystery that made Bébée's heart quicken with expectancy. "Come in; I have something for you. They were my dead daughter's —you have heard me talk of her; Aimée, who died forty year or more ago, they say; for me I think it was yesterday. Trine Krebs—she is a hard woman —heard me talking of my girl. She burst out laughing, 'Lord's sake, fool, why your girl would be sixty now if she had lived.' Well, so it may be; you see, the new mill was put up the week she died, and you call the new mill old; but, my girl, she is young to me. Always young. Come here, Bébée."

Bébée went after him, a little awed, into the

dusky interior, that smelt of stored apples and of dried herbs that hung from the roof. There was a walnut-wood press, such as the peasants of France and the Low Countries keep their homespun linen in, and their old lace that serves for the nuptials and baptisms of half a score of generations.

The old man unlocked it with a trembling hand, and there came from it an odour of dead lavender and of withered rose leaves. On the shelves there were a girl's set of clothes, and a girl's sabots, and a girl's communion veil and wreath.

"They are all hers," he whispered; "all hers. And sometimes in the evening-time I see her coming along the lane for them—do you not know? There is nothing changed; nothing changed; the grass, and the trees, and the huts, and the pond are all here—why should she only be gone away?"

"Antoine is gone."

"Yes. But he was old; my girl is young."

He stood a moment, with the press door open; a perplexed trouble in his dim eyes; the divine faith of love and the mule-like stupidity of ignorance made him cling to this one thought without power of judgment in it.

"They say she would be sixty," he said, with a little dreary smile. "But that is absurd, you know. Why, she had cheeks like yours, and she would run —no lapwing could fly faster over corn. These are her things, you see; yes—all of them. That is the sprig of sweetbriar she wore in her belt the day before the waggon knocked her down and killed her. I have never touched the things. But look here, Bébée, you are a good child and true, and like her just a little. I mean to give you her silver clasps. They were her great-great-great-grandmother's before her. God knows how old they are not. And a girl should have some little wealth of that sort— and for Antoine's sake——"

The old man stayed behind, closing the press-door upon the lavender-scented clothes, and sitting down in the dull shadow of the hut to think of his daughter, dead forty summers and more.

Bébée went out with the brave, broad silver clasps about her waist, and the tears wet on her cheeks for a grief not her own. To be killed just when one was young, and was loved like that, and all the world was in its May-day flower—the silver felt cold to her touch—as cold as though it were the dead girl's hands that held her.

The garlands that the children strung of daisies and hung about her had never chilled her so.

But little Jeanne, the youngest of the charcoal-burner's little tribe, running to meet her, screamed with glee, and danced in the gay morning.

"Oh, Bébée! how you glitter! Did the Virgin send you that off her own altar! Let me see —let me touch! Is it made of the stars or of the sun?"

And Bébée danced with the child, and the silver gleamed and sparkled, and all the people came running out to see, and the milk-carts were half an hour later for town, and the hens cackled loud un-fed, and the men even stopped on their way to the fields and paused, with their scythes on their shoul-ders, to stare at the splendid gift.

"There is not such another set of clasps in Brabant; old work you could make a fortune of in the curiosity shops in the Montagne," said Trine

Krebs, going up the steps of her mill-house, "Yet, all the same, you know, Bébée, things off a dead body bring mischance sometimes."

But Bébée danced with the child, and did not hear.

Whose fête day had ever begun like this one of hers?

She was a little poet at heart, and should not have cared for such vanities; but when one is only sixteen, and has only a little rough woollen frock, and sits in the market-place or the lace-room, with other girls around, how should one be altogether indifferent to a broad, embossed, beautiful shield of silver that sparkles with each step one takes?

A quarter of an hour idle thus was all, however, that Bébée or her friends could spare at five o'clock on a summer morning, when the city was waiting for its eggs, its honey, its flowers, its cream, and its butter, and Tambour was shaking his leather harness in impatience to be off with his milk-cans.

So Bébée, all holiday though it was, and heroine though she felt herself, ran indoors, put up her cakes and cherries, cut her two basketsfull out of the garden, locked her hut, and went on her quick happy little feet along the grassy paths towards the city. The sorting and tying up of the flowers she always left until she was sitting under the awning in front of the Broodhuis; the same awning, tawny as an autumn pear and weather-blown as an old sail, which had served to shelter Antoine Maes from heat and rain, through all the years of his life.

"Go to the Madeleine; you will make money there, with your pretty blue eyes, Bébée," people had said to her of late; but Bébée had shaken her head. Where she had sat in her babyhood at Antoine's feet, she would sit so long as she sold flowers in Brussels—here, underneath the shadow of the Gothic towers that saw Egmont die.

Old Antoine had never gone into the grand market that is fashioned after the Madeleine of Paris, and where in the cool, wet, sweet-smelling halls, all the flowers of Brabant are spread in bouquets fit for the bridal of Una, and large as the shield of the Redcross Knight.

Antoine could not compete with all those treasures of greenhouse and stove. He had always had

his little stall amongst those which spread their
tawny awnings and their merry hardy blossoms under the shadow of the Hôtel de Ville, in the midst
of the buyings and sellings, the games and the
quarrels, the auctions and the Cheap Johns, the
mountebanks and the marriage parties, that daily and
hourly throng the Grande Place.

Here Bébée, from three years old, had been
used to sit beside him, and ponder seriously on
grave and troublesome things, though by nature she
was as gay as a lark.

The people always heard her singing as they
passed the garden. The children never found their
games so merry as when she danced their rounds
with them; and though she dreamed so much out
there in the air amongst the carnations and the
roses, or in the long, low workroom in the town,
high against the crocketed pinnacles of the cathedral
—yet her dreams, if vaguely wistful, were all bright
of hue and sunny in their phantasies—still she had
one unsatisfied and sad desire: she wanted to know
so much, and she knew nothing.

She did not care for the grand and gay people.

When the band played, and the park filled, and
the bright little cafés were thronged with pleasure-
seekers, and the crowds flocked hither and thither
to the woods, to the theatres, to the galleries, to
the guinguettes, Bébée, going gravely along with her
emptied baskets homeward, envied none of these.

When at Noël, the little children hugged their
loads of puppets and sugar-plums; when at the Fête
Dieu, the whole people flocked out be-ribboned and
vari-coloured like any bed of spring-anemones; when
in the merry midsummer the chars-à-bancs trundled
away into the forest with laughing loads of students
and maidens; when in the rough winters the carriages left furred and jewelled women at the doors
of the operas or the palaces—Bébée, going and
coming through the city to her flower-stall or lace-
work, looked at them all, and never thought of envy
or desire.

She had her little hut; she could get her bread;
she lived with the flowers; the neighbours were good
to her, and now and then, on a saint's day, she too

got her day in the woods; it never occurred to her
that her lot could be better.

But sometimes sitting, looking at the dark old
beauty of the Broodhuis, or at the wondrous carven
fronts of other Spanish houses, or at the painted
stories of the cathedral windows, or at the quaint
colours of the shipping on the quay, or at the long,
dark aisles of trees that went away through the
forest to the far Ardennes mountains, where her
steps had never wandered—sometimes Bébée would
get pondering on all this unknown world that lay
before and behind and around her, and a sense of
her own utter ignorance would steal on her; and
she would say to herself; "If only I knew a little—
just a very little!"

But it is not easy to know even a very little
when you have to work for one's bread from sunrise to nightfall, and when none of your friends
know how to read or write; and even your old priest
is one of a family of peasants, and can just teach
you the alphabet, and that is all. For Father Francis
could do no more than this; and all his spare time
was taken up in digging his cabbage plot and see-

ing to his beehives; and the only books that Bébée
ever beheld were a few tattered Lives of Saints that
lay moth-eaten on a shelf of his cottage.

But Brussels has stones that are sermons, or
rather that are quaint, touching, illuminated legends
of the middle ages, which those who run may
read.

Brussels is a gay little city that lies as bright
within its girdle of woodland as any butterfly that
rests upon moss.

The city has its ways and wiles of Paris. It
decks itself with white and gold. It has music
under its trees and soldiers in its streets, and troops
marching and counter-marching along its sunny
avenues. It has blue and pink, and yellow and green,
on its awnings and on its house-fronts. It has a
merry open-air life on its pavements at little marble
tables before little gay-coloured cafés. It has gilded
balconies and tossing flags and comic operas, and
leisurely pleasure-seekers, and tries always to believe
and make the world believe that it is Paris in very
truth.

But this is only the Brussels of the noblesse and the foreigners.

There is a Brussels that is better than this—a Brussels that belongs to the old burgher-life, to the artists and the craftsmen, to the master masons of Moyen-age, to the same spirit and soul that once filled the free men of Ghent and the citizens of Bruges and the besieged of Leyden, and the blood of Egmont and of Horne.

Down there by the water-side, where the old quaint walls lean over the yellow sluggish stream, and the green barrels of the Antwerp barges swing against the dusky piles of the crumbling bridges.

In the grey square desolate courts of the old palaces, where in cobwebbed galleries and silent chambers the Flemish tapestries drop to pieces.

In the great populous square, where, above the clamorous and rushing crowds, the majestic front of the Maison du Roi frowns against the sun, and the spires and pinnacles of the Burgomaster's gathering-halls tower into the sky in all the fantastic luxuriance of Gothic fancy.

Under the vast shadowy wings of angels in the

stillness of the cathedral, across whose sunny aisles some little child goes slowly all alone, laden with lilies for the Feast of the Assumption, till their white glory hides its curly head.

In all strange quaint old world niches withdrawn from men in silent grass-grown corners, where a twelfth-century corbel holds a pot of roses, or a gothic arch yawns beneath a wool-warehouse, or a water-spout with a grinning faun's head laughs in the grim humour of the Moyen-age above the bent head of a young lace-worker.

In all these, Brussels, although more worldly than her sisters of Ghent and Bruges, and far more worldly yet than her Teuton cousins of Freiburg and Nürnberg, Brussels is in her own way still like some monkish story, mixed up with the Romaunt of the Rose, or rather like some light French vaudeville, all jests and smiles, illustrated in motley contrast with helm and hauberk, cope and cowl, praying knights and fighting priests, winged griffins and nimbused saints, flame-breathing dragons and enamoured princes, all mingled together in the illuminated colours and the heroical grotesque romance of the Middle Ages.

And it was this side of the city that Bébée knew, and she loved it well, and would not leave it for the market of the Madeleine.

She had no one to tell her anything, and all Antoine had ever been able to say to her concerning the Broodhuis was that it had been there in his father's time; and regarding Ste. Gudule, that his mother had burned many a candle before its altars for a dead brother who had been drowned off the dunes.

But the child's mind unled, but not misled, had pondered on these things, and her heart had grown to love them; and perhaps no student of Spanish architecture, no antiquary of Moyen-age relics, loved Ste. Gudule and the Broodhuis as little ignorant Bébée did.

There had been a time when great dark fierce men had builded these things, and made the place beautiful. So much she knew; and the little wistful, untaught intelligence tried to project itself into

those unknown times, and failed, and yet found
pleasure in the effort.

And Bébée would say to herself as she walked
the streets—

"Perhaps some one will come some day who will
tell me all those things."

Meanwhile, there were the flowers, and she was
quite content.

Besides, she knew all the people: the old cobbler who sat next her, and chattered all day long
like a magpie; the tinker, who had come up many
a summer night to drink a glass with Antoine; the
cheap John, who cheated everybody, but who had
always given her a toy or a trinket at every Fête
Dieu all the summers she had known; the little old
woman, sour as a crab, who sold rosaries and pictures of saints, and little waxen Christs upon a tray;
the big dogs who pulled the carts in and lay pant-
ing all day under the rush-bottomed chairs on
which the egg-wives and the fruit-sellers sat, and
knitted, and chaffered; nay, even the gorgeous huis-
sier and the frowning gendarme, who marshalled

the folks into order as they went up for municipal registries, or for street-misdemeanours.

She knew them all; had known them all ever since she had first trotted in like a little dog at Antoine's heels.

So Bébée stayed there.

It is, perhaps, the most beautiful square in all Northern Europe, with its black timbers and gilded carvings, and blazoned windows, and majestic scutcheons, and fantastic pinnacles. This Bébée did not know, but she loved it, and she sat resolutely in front of the Broodhuis, selling her flowers, smiling, chatting, helping the old woman, counting her little gains, eating her bit of bread at noonday like any other market girl, but, at times, glancing up to the stately towers and the blue sky, with a look on her face that made the old tinker and cobbler whisper together—"What does she see there? —the dead people or the angels?"

The truth was that even Bébée herself did not know very surely what she saw—something that was still nearer to her than even this kindly crowd that loved her. That was all she could have said had anybody asked her.

But none did.

No one wanted to hear what the dead said; and for the angels, the tinker and the cobbler were of opinion that one had only too much of them sculptured about everywhere, and shining on all the casements—in reverence, be it spoken of course.

———

## CHAPTER III.

"I REMEMBERED it was your name-day, child. Here are half-a-dozen eggs," said one of the hen-wives, and the little cross woman with the pedlar's tray, added a waxen St. Agnes, coloured red and yellow to the very life, no doubt; and Père Melchior, the sweetmeat sellèr, brought her a gilded horn of comfits; and the old cheap John had saved her a. cage for the starling; and the tinker had a cream cheese for her in a vine-leaf, and the cobbler had made her, actually, a pair of shoes—red shoes, beautiful shoes to go to mass in, and be a wonder in to all the neighbourhood. And they thronged round her, and adored the silver waist buckles; and when Bébée got fairly to her stall and traffic began, she thought once more that nobody's feast-day had ever dawned like hers.

When the chimes began to ring all over the city, she could hardly believe that the carillon was

not saying its "Laus Deo" with some special meaning in its bells for her.

The morning went by as usual; the noise of
the throngs about her like a driving of angry winds,
but no more hurting her than the angels on the
roof of Ste. Gudule are hurt by the storm when it
breaks.

Hard words, fierce passions, low thoughts, evil
deeds, passed by the child without resting on her;
her heart was in her flowers, and was like one of
them, with the dew of daybreak on it.

There were many strangers in the city, and such
are always sure to loiter in the Spanish square;
and she sold fast and well her lilacs and her roses,
and her knots of thyme and sweetbriar. She was
always a little sorry to see them go, her kindly
pretty playmates that, nine times out of ten, no
doubt, only drooped and died in the hands that
purchased them, as human souls soil and shrivel in
the grasp of the passions that woo them.

The day was a busy one, and brought in good
profit. Bébée had no less than fifty sous in her
leather pouch when it was over; a sum of magni-

tude in the green lane by Laeken. A few of her moss roses were still unsold, that was all, when the Ave Maria began ringing over the town, and the people dispersed to their homes or their pleasuring.

It was a warm grey evening, the streets were full; there were blossoms in all the balconies, and gay colours in all the dresses. The old tinker put his tools together and whispered to her—

"Bébée, as it is your feast-day, come and stroll in St. Hubert's gallery, and I will buy you a horn of sugar-plums or a ribbon, and we can see the puppet-show afterwards, eh?"

But the children were waiting at home: she would not spend the evening in the city; she only thought she would just kneel a moment in the cathedral and say a little prayer or two for a minute —the saints were so good in giving her so many friends.

There is something very touching in the Netherlander's relation with his Deity. It is all very vague to him; a jumble of veneration and familiarity, of

4*

sanctity and profanity, without any thought of being familiar, or any idea of being profane.

There is a homely poetry, an innocent affectionateness, in it characteristic of the people.

He talks to his good angel Michel, and to his friend that dear little Jesus, much as he would talk to the shoemaker over the way, or the cooper's child in the doorway.

It is a very unreasonable, foolish, clumsy sort of religion, this theology in wooden shoes; it is half grotesque, half pathetic; the grandmothers pass it on to the grandchildren, as they pass the bowl of potatoes round the stove in the long winter nights; it is as silly as possible, but it comforts them as they carry faggots over the frozen canals or wear their eyes blind over the squares of lace; and it has in it the supreme pathos of a perfect confidence, of an utter childlike and undoubting trust.

This had been taught to Bébée, and she went to sleep every night in the firm belief that the sixteen little angels of the Flemish prayer kept watch and ward over her bed.

For the rest, being poetical, as Netherlanders are not, and having in her—wherever it came from, poor little soul—a warmth of fancy and a spirituality of vision not at all northern, she had mixed up her religion with the fairies of Antoine's stories, and the demons in which the Flemish folk are profound believers, and the flowers, into which she put all manner of sentient life, until 'it was a fantastic medley so entangled, that poor Father Francis had given up in despair any attempt to arrange it more correctly.

Indeed, being of the peasantry himself, he was not so very full sure in his own mind that demons were not bodily presences, quite as real and often much more tangible than saints.  Any way he let her alone; and only taught her to believe in the goodness of God as in the shining of the stars.

People looked after her as she went through the twisting, picture-like streets, where sunlight fell still between the peaked high roofs, and lamps were here and there lit in the bric-à-brac shops and the fruit-stalls.

Her little muslin cap blew back like the wings

of a white butterfly. Her sunny hair caught the last sun-rays. Her feet were fair in the brown wooden shoes. Under the short woollen skirts the grace of her pretty limbs moved freely. Her broad silver clasps shone like a shield, and she was utterly unconscious that anyone looked; she was simply and gravely intent on reaching Ste. Gudule to say her one prayer and not keep the children waiting.

Some one leaning idly over a balcony in the street that is named after Mary of Burgundy saw her going thus. He left the balcony and went down his stairs and followed her.

The sun dazzle on the silver had first caught his sight; and then he had looked downward at the pretty feet. These are the chances that women call Fate.

Bébée entered the cathedral. It was quite empty. Far away at the west end there was an old custodian asleep on a bench, and a woman kneeling. That was all.

Bébée made her salutations to the high altar, and stole on into the chapel of the Saint Sacrament; it was that one that she loved best.

She said her prayer, and thanked the saints for all their gifts and goodness, her clasped hands against her silver shield; her basket on the pavement by her; abovehead the sunset rays streaming purple and crimson and golden through the painted windows that are the wonder of the world.

When her prayer was done she still kneeled there; her head thrown back to watch the light; her hands clasped still; and on her upturned face the look that made the people say, "What does she see?—the angels or the dead?"

She forgot everything. She forgot the cherries at home, and the children even. She was looking upward at the stories of the painted panes; she was listening to the message of the dying sunrays; she was feeling vaguely, wistfully, unutterably the tender beauty of the sacred place and the awful wonder of the world in which she with her sixteen years was all alone, like a little blue cornflower amongst the wheat that goes for grist, and the barley that makes men drunk.

For she was alone, though she had so many friends. Quite alone sometimes for God had been cruel to her, and had made her a lark without song.

When the sun faded and the beautiful casements lost all glow and meaning, Bébée rose with a startled look—had she been dreaming?—was it night?—would the children be sorry, and go supperless to bed?

"Have you a rosebud left to sell to me?" a man's voice said not far off; it was low and sweet as became the Sacrament Chapel. Bébée looked up; she did not quite know what she saw; only dark eyes smiling into hers. By the instinct of habit she sought in her basket and found three moss-roses. She held them out to him.

"I do not sell flowers here, but I will *give* them to you," she said, in her pretty grave childish fashion.

"I often want flowers," said the stranger, as he took the buds. "Where do you sell yours?—in the market?"

"In the Grande Place."

"Will you tell me your name, pretty one?"

"I am Bébée."

There were people coming into the church. The bells were booming abovehead for vespers. There was a shuffle of chairs and a stir of feet. Boys in white went to and fro, lighting the candles. Great clouds of shadow drifted up into the roof and hid the angels.

She nodded her little head to him.

"Good-night—I cannot stay—I have a cake at home to-night, and the children are waiting."

"Ah! that is important, no doubt, indeed. Will you buy some more cakes for the children from me?"

He slid a gold piece in her hand. She looked at it in amaze. In the green lanes by Laeken no one ever saw gold. Then she gave it him back.

"I will not take money in church, nor anywhere, except what the flowers are worth. Goodnight."

He followed her, and held back the heavy oak door for her, and went out into the air with her.

It was dark already, but in the square there was still the cool bright primrose-coloured evening light.

Bébée's wooden shoes went pattering down the sloping and uneven stones. Her little grey figure ran quickly through the deep shade cast from the towers and walls. Her dreams had drifted away. She was thinking of the children and the cake.

"You are in such a hurry because of the cake?" said her new customer, as he followed her.

Bébée looked back at him with a smile in her blue eyes.

"Yes—they will be waiting, you know, and there are cherries too."

"It is a grand day with you, then?"

"It is my fête-day: I am sixteen."

She was proud of this. She told it to the very dogs in the street.

"Ah!—you feel old, I dare say?"

"Oh, quite old! They cannot call me a child any more."

"Of course not. It would be ridiculous. Are those presents in your basket?"

"Yes, every one of them." She paused a moment to lift the dead vine-leaves, and show him the beautiful shining red shoes. "Look!—old

Gringoire gave me these. I shall wear them at mass next Sunday. I never had a pair of shoes in my life."

"But how will you wear shoes without stockings?"

It was a snake cast into her Eden.

She had never thought of it.

"Perhaps I can save money and buy some," she answered, after a sad little pause. "But that I could not do till next year. They would cost several francs, I suppose."

"Unless a good fairy gives them to you?"

Bébée smiled; fairies were real things to her—relations indeed. She did not imagine that he spoke in jest.

"Sometimes I pray very much and things come," she said softly. "When the Gloire de Dijon rose-tree was cut back too soon one summer, and never blossomed, and we all thought it was dead, I prayed all day long for it, and never thought of anything else, and by autumn it was all in new leaf, and now its flowers are finer than ever."

"But you watered it whilst you prayed, I suppose?"

The sarcasm escaped her.

She was wondering to herself whether it would
be vain and wicked to pray for a pair of stockings: she thought she would go and ask Father
Francis.

By this time they were in the Rue Royale, and
half way down it. The lamps were lighted. A
regiment was marching up it with a band playing.
The windows were open, and people were laughing
and singing in some of them. The light caught
the white and gilded fronts of the houses. The
pleasure-seeking crowds loitered along in the warmth
of the evening.

Bébée, suddenly roused from her thoughts by
the loud challenge of the military music, looked
round on the stranger, and motioned him back.

"Sir;—I do not know you—why should you
come with me? Do not do it, please. You make
me talk, and that makes me late."

And she pushed her basket farther on her arm,

and nodded to him, and ran off—as fleetly as a hare through fern—amongst the press of the people.

"To-morrow, little one," he answered her with a careless smile, and let her go unpursued. Above, from the open casement of a café, some young men and some painted women leaned out, and threw sweetmeats at him, as in carnival time.

"A new model, Flamen, that pretty peasant?" they asked him.

He laughed in answer, and went up the steps to join them: he dropped the moss-roses as he went, and trod on them, and did not wait.

Bébée ran home as fast as her feet would take her.

The children were all gathered about her gate in the dusky, dewy evening; they met her with shouts of welcome and reproach intermingled; they had been watching for her since first the sun had grown low and red, and now the moon was risen.

But they forgave her when they saw the splendour of her presents, and she showered out amongst them Père Melchior's horn of comfits.

They dashed into the hut; they dragged the one

little table out amongst the flowers; the cherries
and cake were spread on it; and the miller's wife
had given a big jug of milk, and Father Francis
himself had sent some honeycomb.

The early roses were full of scent in the dew;
the great gillyflowers breathed out fragrance in the
dusk; the goat came and nibbled the sweetbriar
unrebuked; the children repeated the Flemish bread-
grace, with clasped hands and reverent eyes—"Oh,
dear little Jesus, come and sup with us, and bring
your beautiful Mother too; we will not forget you
are God." Then that said, they ate, and drank,
and laughed, and picked cherries from each other's
mouths like little blackbirds; the big white dog
gnawed a crust at their feet; old Krebs, who had a
fiddle, and could play it, came out and trilled them
rude and ready Flemish tunes, such as Teniers or
Mieris might have jumped to before an ale-house
at Kermesse. Bébée and the children joined hands,
and danced round together in the broad white
moonlight, on the grass, by the water-side; the
idlers came and sat about, the women netting or
spinning, and the men smoking a pipe before bed-

time; the rough hearty Flemish bubbled like a brook in gossip, or rung like a horn over a jest; Bébée and the children, tired of their play, grew quiet, and chaunted together the "Ave Maria Stella Virginis;" a nightingale amongst the willows sang to the sleeping swans.

All was happy, quiet, homely; lovely also in its simple way. They went early to their beds, as people must do who rise at dawn.

Bébée leaned out a moment from her own little casement, ere she too went to rest.

Through an open lattice there sounded the murmur of some little child's prayer; the wind sighed amongst the willows; the nightingales sang on in the dark—all was still.

Hard work awaited her on the morrow, and on all the other days of the year.

She was only a little peasant; she must sweep, and spin, and dig, and delve, to get daily her bit of black bread; but that night she was as happy as a little princess in a fairy tale; happy in her playmates, in her flowers, in her sixteen years, in her red shoes, in her silver buckles, happy in the dewy

leaves, in the singing birds, in the hush of the
night, in the sense of rest, in the fragrance of
flowers, in the drifting changes of moon and cloud,
happy because she was half a woman, because she
was half a poet, because she was wholly a child.

"Oh, dear swans, how good it is to be sixteen!
—how good it is to live at all!—do you not tell
the willows so!" said Bébée to the gleam of silver
under the dark leaves by the water's side, which
showed her where her friends were sleeping, with
their snowy wings closed over their stately heads,
and the veiled gold and ruby of their eyes.

The swans did not awake to answer.

Only the nightingale answered from the willows, with Desdemona's song.

But Bébée had never heard of Desdemona, and
the willows had no sigh for her.

"Good-night!" she said, softly, to all the green
dewy sleeping world, and then she lay down and
slept herself:—the nightingale sang on, and the willows trembled.

## CHAPTER VI.

"If I could save a centime a day, I could buy a pair of stockings this time next year," thought Bébée, locking her shoes with her other treasures in her drawer the next morning, and taking her broom and pail to wash down her little palace.

But a centime a day is a great deal in Brabant, when one has not always enough for bare bread, and when, in the long chill winter, one must weave thread lace all through the short daylight for next to nothing at all, for there are so many women in Brabant, and every one of them, young or old, can make lace, and if one do not like the pitiful wage, one may leave it and go and die, for what the master lace-makers care or know; there will always be enough, many more than enough, to twist the thread round the bobbins, and weave the bridal veils, and the trains for the courts.

"And besides, if I can save a centime, Varnhart

ought to have it," thought Bébée, as she swept the dust together.

It was so selfish of her to be dreaming about a pair of stockings, when those little things often went for days on a stew of nettles.  So she looked at her own pretty feet—pretty, and slender, and arched, rosy and fair, and uncramped by the pressure of leather,—and resigned her day-dream with a brave heart, as she put up her broom, and went out to weed, and hoe, and trim, and prune the garden that had been for once neglected the night before.

"One could not move half so easily in stockings," she thought, with wise philosophy, as she worked amongst the black fresh sweet-smelling mould, and kissed a rose now and then as she passed one.

When she got into the city that day, her rush-bottomed chair, which was always left upside down in case rain should fall in the night, was set ready for her, and on its seat was a gay, gilded box, such as rich people give away full of bonbons at the New Year.

Bébée stood and looked from the box to the Broodhuis, from the Broodhuis to the box; she glanced around, but no one had come there so early as she, except the tinker, who was busy quarrelling with his wife, and letting his smelting fire burn a hole in his breeches.

The box was certainly for her, since it was set upon her chair?—Bébée pondered a moment; then little by little opened the lid.

Within, on a nest of rose satin, were two pair of silk stockings!—Real silk!—with the prettiest clocks worked up their sides in colour!

Bébée gave a little scream, and stood still, the blood hot in her cheeks; no one heard her, the tinker's wife, who alone was near, having just wished heaven to send a judgment on her husband, was busy putting out his smoking small-clothes. It is a way that women and wives have, and they never see the bathos of it.

The Place filled gradually.

The customary crowds gathered. The business of the day began underneath the multitudinous tones of the chiming bells. Bébée's business began

5*

too; she put the box behind her with a beating heart, and tied up her flowers.

It was the fairies, of course!—but they had never set a rush-bottomed chair on its legs before, and this action of theirs frightened her.

It was rather an empty morning. She sold little, and there was the more time to think.

About an hour after noon, a voice addressed her,—

"Have you three more moss roses for me?"

Bébée looked up with a smile and found some. It was her companion of the Cathedral. She had thought much of the red shoes, and the silver clasps, but she had thought nothing at all of him.

"You are not too proud to be paid to-day?" he said, giving her a silver franc—he would not alarm her with any more gold; she thanked him, and slipped it in her little leathern pouch, and went on sorting some clove pinks.

"You do not seem to remember me?" he said, with a little sadness.

"Oh, I remember you," said Bébée, lifting her

frank eyes. "But you know I speak to so many people, and they are all nothing to me."

"Who is anything to you?"

It was softly and insidiously spoken, but it awoke no echo.

"Varnhart's children," she answered him, instantly. "And dear old Annémie by the wharfside; and Tambour—and Antoine's grave—and the starling—and, of course, above all, the flowers."

"And the fairies, I suppose?—though they do nothing for you."

She looked at him eagerly,—

"They have done something to-day. I have found a box, and some stockings—such beautiful stockings! Silk ones! Is it not very odd?"

"It is more odd they should have forgotten you so long. May I see them?"

"I cannot show them to you now. Those ladies are going to buy. But you can see them later—if you wait."

"I will wait and paint the Broodhuis."

"So many people do that; you are a painter then?"

"Yes—in a way."

He sat down on an edge of the stall, and spread his things there, and sketched, whilst the traffic went on around them. He was very many years older than she; handsome, with a dark, and changeful, and listless face; he wore brown velvet, and had a red ribbon at his throat; he looked a little as Egmont might have done when wooing Claire.

Bébée, as she sold the flowers, and took the change fifty times in the hour, looked at him now and then, and watched the movements of his hands —she could not have told why.

Always amongst men and women—always in the crowds of the streets—people were nothing to her; she went through them as through a field of standing corn; only in the field she would have tarried for poppies, and in the town she tarried for no one.

She dealt with men as with women, simply, truthfully, frankly, with the innocent fearlessness of a child; when they told her she was pretty, she smiled; it was just as they said that her flowers were sweet.

But this one's hands moved so swiftly, and as she saw her Broodhuis growing into colour and form beneath them she could not choose but look now and then, and twice she gave her change wrong.

He spoke to her rarely, and sketched on and on in rapid bold strokes the quaint graces and massive richness of the Maison du Roi.

There is no crowd so busy in Brabant that it will not find leisure to stare. The Fleming has nothing of the Frenchman's courtesy; he is rough and rude; he remains a peasant even when town-bred, and the surly insolence of the "Gueux" is in him still; he is kindly to his fellows, though not to beasts; he is shrewd, patient, thrifty, industrious, and good in very many ways, but civil never.

A good score of them left off their occupations and clustered round the painter, staring, chatter-ing, pushing, pointing, as though a brush had never been seen in all the land of Rubens.

Bébée, ashamed of her people, got up from her chair and rebuked them.

"Oh, men of Brussels; fie then for shame!" she called to them as clearly as a robin sings. "Did never you see a drawing before? and are there not brave pictures to see in the galleries, St. Lieven and Our Lady, and all? and have you never some better thing to do than to gape wide-mouthed at a stranger? What laziness—ah! just worthy of a people who sleep and smoke while their dogs work for them! Go away, all of you; look, there comes the gendarme—it will be the worse for you. Sir— if you sit under my stall; they will not dare trouble you then."

He moved under the awning, thanking her with a smile, and the people, laughing, shuffled unwillingly aside and let him paint on in peace.

It was only little Bébée, but they had spoilt the child from her infancy, and were used to obey her.

The painting took a long time. He set about it with the bold ease of one used to all the intricacies of form and colour, and he had the skill of a master. But he spent more than half the time looking idly at the humours of the populace or watching how the treasures of Bébée's garden went away one by one in the hands of strangers.

Meanwhile, ever and again, sitting on the edge of her stall, with his colours and brushes tossed out on the board, he talked to her, and with the soft imperceptible skill of long practice in those arts, he drew out the details of her little simple life.

There were not always people to buy, and whilst she rested and sheltered the flowers from the sun, she answered him willingly, and in one of her longer rests showed him the wonderful stockings.

"Do you think it *could* be the fairies?" she asked him a little doubtfully.

It was easy to make her believe any fantastical nonsense; but her fairies were ethereal divinities. She could scarcely believe that they had laid that box on her chair.

"Impossible to doubt it!" he replied, unhesitatingly. "Given a belief in fairies at all, why should there be any limit to what they can do? It is the same with the saints, is it not?"

"Yes," said Bébée, thoughtfully.

The saints were mixed up in her imagination with the fairies in an intricacy that would have defied the best reasonings of Father Francis.

"Well, then, you will wear the stockings, will you not? Only believe me, your feet are far prettier without them."

Bébée laughed happily and took another peep in the cosy rose-satin nest. But her little face had a certain perplexity. Suddenly she turned on him.

"Did not *you* put them there?"

"I?—never!"

"Are you quite sure?"

"Quite; but why ask?"

"Because," said Bébée, shutting the box resolutely and pushing it a little away, "because I would not take it if you did. You are a stranger, and a present is a debt, so Antoine always said."

"Why take a present then from the Varnhart children, or your old friend who gave you the clasps?"

"Ah, that is very different. When people are
very, very poor, equally poor, the one with the
other, little presents that they save for and make
with such a difficulty, are just things that are a
pleasure; sacrifices; like your sitting up with a sick
person at night, and then she sits up with you
another year when you want it. Do you not
know?"

"I know you talk very prettily. But why should
you not take any one else's present, though he may
not be poor?"

"Because I could not return it."

"Could you not?"

The smile in his eyes dazzled her a little; it
was so strange, and yet had so much light in it;
but she did not understand him one whit.

"No; how could I?" she said, earnestly. "If I
were to save for two years, I could not get francs
enough to buy anything worth giving back; and I
should be so unhappy, thinking of the debt of it
always. Do tell me if you put those stockings
there?"

"No;" he looked at her and the trivial lie faltered and died away; the eyes, clear as crystal, questioned him so innocently.

"Well, if I did!" he said, frankly, "you wished for them; what harm was there! Will you be so cruel as to refuse them from me?"

The tears sprang into Bébée's eyes. She was sorry to lose the beautiful box, but more sorry he had lied to her.

"It was very kind and good," she said, regretfully. "But I cannot think why you should have done it, as you had never known me at all. And, indeed, I could not take them, because Antoine would not let me if he were alive; and if I gave you a flower every day all the year round, I should not pay you the worth of them—it would be quite impossible; and why should you tell me falsehoods about such a thing! A falsehood is never a thing for a man."

She shut the box and pushed it towards him, and turned to the selling of her bouquets. Her voice shook a little as she tied up a bunch of mignonette and told the price of it. Those beautiful stockings! why had she ever seen them, and why had he told her a lie?

It made her heart heavy. For the first time in her brief life the Broodhuis seemed to frown between her and the sun. Undisturbed he painted on and did not look at her.

The day was nearly done. The people began to scatter. The shadows grew very long. He painted on, not glancing once elsewhere than at his study. Bébée's baskets were quite empty.

She rose, and lingered, and regarded him wistfully: he was angered; perhaps she had been rude? Her little heart failed her.

If he would only look up?——

But he did not look up; he kept his handsome dark face studiously over the canvas of the Broodhuis. She would have seen a smile in his eyes if he had lifted them; but he never raised his lids.

Bébée hesitated: take the stockings she would not; but perhaps she had refused them too roughly. She wished so that he would look up and save her speaking first; but he knew what he was about too warily and well to help her thus.

She waited awhile, then took one little red moss rosebud that she had saved all day in a corner of her basket, and held it out to him frankly, shyly, as a peace offering.

"Was I rude? I did not mean to be. But I cannot take the stockings; and why did you tell me that falsehood?"

He took the rosebud and got up too, and smiled; but he did not meet her eyes.

"Let us forget the whole matter; it is not worth a sou. If you do not take the box, leave it; it is of no use to me."

"I cannot take it."

She knew she was doing right. How was it that he could make her feel as though she were acting wrongly?

"Leave it, then, I say. You are not the first woman, my dear, who has quarrelled with a wish fulfilled. It is a way your sex has, of rewarding gods and men. Here, you old witch—here is a

treasure trove for you.   You can sell it for ten
francs in the town anywhere."

As he spoke he tossed the casket and the stockings in it to an old decrepit woman, who was
passing by with a baker's cart, drawn by a dog; and
not staying to heed her astonishment, gathered his
colours and easel together.

The tears swam in Bébée's eyes as she saw the
box whirled through the air.

She had done right—she was sure she had done
right.   He was a stranger, and she could never
have repaid him; but he made her feel herself
wayward and ungrateful, and it was hard to see the
beautiful fairy gift borne away for ever by the
chuckling, hobbling, greedy old bread-woman.   If
he had only taken it himself, she would have been
glad then to have been brave and to have done her
duty.

But it was not in his design that she should be
glad.

He saw her tears, but he seemed not to see
them.

"Good-night, Bébée," he said carelessly, as he

sauntered aside from her. "Good-night, my dear. To-morrow I will finish my painting; but I will not offend you by any more gifts."

Bébée lifted her drooped head, and looked him in the eyes eagerly, with a certain sturdy resolve and timid wistfulness intermingled in her look.

"Sir, you speak to me quite wrongly," she said with a quick accent, that had pride as well as pain in it. "Say it was kind to bring me what I wished for—yes, it was kind, I know—but you told me a lie about it, and that is a cowardly thing, and, indeed, had no sense whatever in it. Besides you never saw me till last night, and I cannot tell even your name; and I am only Bébée, and cannot give you anything back, because I have only just enough to feed myself and the starling, and not always that in winter. I thank you very much for what you wished to do; but if I had taken those things, I think you would have thought me very mean and full of greed; and Antoine always said, 'Do not take what you cannot pay—not ever what you cannot pay— that is the way to walk with pure feet.' Perhaps I spoke ill, because they spoil me, and they say I am

too swift to say my mind. But I am not thankless
—not thankless, indeed—it is only I could not take
what I cannot pay. That is all. You are angry
still—not now—no!"

There was anxiety in the pleading. What did
it matter to her what a stranger thought? And yet
Bébée's heart was heavy as she went out of the city
homewards. He had only laughed a little coldly,
and bade her good-night, and left the square. A
sense of having done wrong weighed on her; of
having been rude and ungrateful.

She had no heart for the children that evening.
Mère Krebs was sitting out before her door shell-
ing peas, and called to her to come in and have a
drop of coffee. Krebs had come in from Vilvöorde
fair, and brought a stock of rare good berries with
him. But Bébée thanked her, and went on to her
own garden to work.

She had always liked to sit out on the quaint
wooden steps of the mill and under the red shadow
of the sails, watching the swallows flutter to and
fro in the sunset, and hearing the droll frogs croak
in the rushes, while the old people told her tales of

the time when in their babyhood they had run out, fearful yet fascinated, to see the beautiful Scots Greys flash by in the murky night, and the endless line of guns and caissons crawl black as a snake through the summer dust, and the trampled corn, going out past the woods to Waterloo.

But to-night she had no fancy for it: she wanted to be alone with the flowers.

Though, to be sure, they had been very heartless when Antoine's coffin had gone past them, still they had sympathy; the daisies smiled at her with their golden eyes, and the roses dropped tears on her hand, just as her mood might be; the flowers were closer friends, after all, than any human souls; and besides, she could say so much to them!

Flowers belong to fairyland; the flowers and the birds, and the butterflies, are all that the world has kept of its golden age; the only perfectly beautiful things on earth, joyous, innocent, half divine, useless, say they who are wiser than God.

Bébée went home and worked among her flowers.

A little laborious figure, with her petticoats twisted high, and her feet wet with the night dews and her back bowed to the hoeing and clipping and raking amongst the blossoming plants.

"How late you are working to-night, Bébée!" one or two called out, as they passed the gate. She looked up and smiled; but went on working while the white moon rose.

She did not know what ailed her.

She went to bed without supper, leaving her bit of bread and bowl of goat's milk to make a meal for the fowls in the morning.

"Little ugly, shameful, naked feet!" she said to them, sitting on the edge of her mattress, and looking at them in the moonlight. They were very pretty feet, and would not have been half so pretty in silk hose and satin shoon; but she did not know that: he had told her she wanted those vanities.

She sat still a long while, her rosy feet swaying to and fro like two roses that grow on one stalk, and hang down in the wind. The little lattice was open; the sweet and dusky garden was beyond; there was a hand's breadth of sky, in which a single star was shining; the leaves of the vine hid all the rest.

6*

But for once she saw none of it.

She only saw the black Broodhuis; the red and gold sunset overhead; the grey stones, with the fallen roseleaves and crushed fruits; and in the shadows two dark, reproachful eyes, that looked at hers.

Had she been grateful?

The little tender, honest heart of hers was troubled and oppressed. For once, that night she slept ill.

———

## CHAPTER V.

ALL the next day she sat under the yellow awning, but she sat alone.

It was market day; there were many strangers. Flowers were in demand. The copper pieces were ringing against one another all the hours through in her leathern bag. The cobbler was in such good humour that he forgot to quarrel with his wife. The fruit was in such plenty that they gave her a leaf-full of white and red currants for her noon-day dinner. And the people split their sides at the Cheap John's jokes; he was so droll. No one saw the leaks in his kettles, or the hole in his bellows, or the leg that was lacking to his milking-stool.

Everybody was gay and merry that day; but Bébée's blue eyes looked wistfully over the throng, and did not find what they sought. Somehow the day seemed dull, and the square empty.

The stones and the timbers around seemed more

than ever full of a thousand stories that they would not tell her because she knew nothing, and was only Bébée.

She had never known a dull hour before. She, a little bright, industrious gay thing, whose hands were always full of work, and whose head was always full of fancies, even in the grimmest winter time, when she wove the lace in the grey, chilly workroom, with the frost on the casements, and the mice running out in their hunger over the bare brick floor.

That bare room was a sad enough place sometimes, when the old women would bewail how they starved on the pittance they gained, and the young women sighed for their aching heads and their failing eyesight, and the children dropped great tears on the bobbins, because they had come out without a crust to break their fast.

She had been sad there often for others, but she had never been dull — not with this unfamiliar, desolate, dreary dulness, that seemed to take all the mirth out of the busy life around her, and all the colour out of the blue sky above. Why, she had no idea herself. She wondered if she were going to be ill; she had never been ill in her life; being strong as a little bird that has never known cage or captivity.

When the day was done, Bébée gave a quick sigh as she looked across the square. She had so wanted to tell him that she was not ungrateful, and she had a little moss rose ready, with a sprig of sweetbriar, and a tiny spray of maiden-hair fern that grew under the willows, which she had kept covered up with a leaf of sycamore all the day long.

No one would have it now.

The child went out of the place sadly, as the carillon rang. There was only the moss rose in her basket, and the red and white currants that had been given her for her dinner.

She went along the twisting, many-coloured, quaintly-fashioned streets, till she came to the waterside.

It is very ancient, there still; there are all manner of old buildings, black and brown and grey, peaked roofs, gabled windows, arched doors, crumbling bridges, twisted galleries leaning to touch the

dark surface of the canal, dusky wharves crowded
with barrels, and bales, and cattle, and timber, and
all the various freightage that the good ships come
and go with all the year round, to and from the
Zuyder Zee, and the Baltic water, and the wild
Northumbrian shores, and the iron-bound Scottish
headlands, and the pretty grey, Norman seaports,
and the white sandy dunes of Holland, with the toy
towns and the straight poplar trees.

Bébée was fond of watching the brigs and barges,
that looked so big to her, with their national flags
flying, and their tall masts standing thick as grass,
and their tawny sails flapping in the wind, and about
them the sweet, strong smell of that strange, unknown thing, the sea.

Sometimes the sailors would talk with her; sometimes some old salt, sitting astride of a cask, would
tell her a mariner's tale of far-away lands and
mysteries of the deep; sometimes some curly-headed
cabin-boy would give her a shell or a plume of
seaweed, and try and make her understand what
the wonderful wild water was like, which was not
quiet and sluggish and dusky as this canal was, but

was for ever changing and moving, and curling and
leaping, and making itself now blue as her eyes,
now black as that thunder-cloud, now white as the
snow that the winter wind tossed, now pearl-hued
and opaline as the convolvulus that blew in her
own garden.

And Bébée would listen, with the shell in her
lap, and try to understand, and gaze at the ships
and then at the sky beyond them, and try to figure
to herself those strange countries, to which these
ships were always going, and saw in fancy all the
blossoming orchard province of green France, and
all the fir-clothed hills and rushing rivers of the
snow-locked Swedish shore, and saw too, doubtless,
many lands that had no place at all except in dream-
land, and were more beautiful even than the beauty
of the earth, as poets' countries are, to their own
sorrow, oftentimes.

But this dull day Bébée did not go down upon
the wharf; she did not want the sailors' tales; she
saw the masts and the bits of bunting that streamed
from them, and they made her restless, which they
had never done before.  Instead she went in at a

dark old door and climbed up a steep staircase that
went up and up and up, as though she were mounting Ste. Gudule's belfry towers; and at the top of
it entered a little chamber in the roof, where one
square unglazed hole that served for light looked
out upon the canal, with all its crowded craft, from
the dainty schooner yacht, fresh as gilding and
holystone could make her, that was running for
pleasure to the Scheldt, to the rude, clumsy coal-
barge, black as night, that bore the rough diamonds
of Belgium to the snow-buried roofs of Christiania
and Stromsöon.

In the little dark attic there was a very old
woman in a red petticoat and a high cap, who sat
against the window, and pricked out lace patterns
with a pin on thick paper. She was eighty-five
years old, and could hardly keep body and soul
together.

Bébée, running to her, kissed her.

"Oh mother Annémie, look here! Beautiful red
and white currants, and a roll; I saved them for
you. They are the first currants we have seen this
year. Me? oh, for me, I have eaten more than are

good! You know I pick fruit like a sparrow, always. Dear mother Annémie, are you better? Are you quite sure you are better to-day?"

The little old withered woman, brown as a walnut and meagre as a rush, took the currants, and smiled with a childish glee, and began to eat them, blessing the child with each crumb she broke off the bread.

"Why had you not a grandmother of your own, my little one?" she mumbled. "How good you would have been to her, Bébée!"

"Yes," said Bébée seriously, but her mind could not grasp the idea. It was easier for her to believe the fanciful lily-parentage of Antoine's stories. "How much work have you done, Annémie? Oh, all that! all that! But there is enough for a week. You work too early and too late, you dear Annémie."

"Nay, Bébée, when one has to get one's bread, that cannot be. But I am afraid my eyes are failing. That rose now, is it well done?"

"Beautifully done. Would the Baës take them

if they were not? You know he is one that cuts every centime in four pieces."

"Ah! sharp enough, sharp enough—that is true. But I am always afraid of my eyes. I do not see the flags out there so well as I used to do."

"Because the sun is so bright, Annémie; that is all. I myself, when I have been sitting all day in the Palace in the light, the flowers look pale to me. And you know it is not age with *me*, Annémie?"

The old woman and the young girl laughed together at that droll idea.

"You have a merry heart, dear little one," said old Annémie. "The saints keep it to you always."

"May I tidy the room a little?"

"To be sure, dear, and thank you too. I have not much time, you see; and somehow my back aches badly when I stoop."

"And it is so damp here for you, over all that water!" said Bébée, as she swept and dusted and set to rights the tiny place, and put in a little broken pot a few sprays of honeysuckle and rose-mary that she had brought with her. "It is so damp here. You should have come and lived in my hut with me, Annémie, and sat out under the vine all day, and looked after the chickens for me when I was in the town. They are such mischievous little souls; as soon as my back is turned one or other is sure to push through the roof, and get out amongst the flower-beds. Will you never change your mind, and live with me, Annémie? I am sure you would be happy, and the starling says your name quite plain, and he is such a funny bird to talk to; you never would tire of him. Will you never come? It is so bright there, and green and sweet smelling, and to think you never even have seen it!—and the swans and all,—it is a shame."

"No, dear," said old Annémie, eating her last bunch of currants. "You have said so so often, and you are good and mean it, that I know. But I could not leave the water. It would kill me.

"Out of this window you know I saw my Jeannot's brig go away—away—away—till the masts were lost in the mists. Going with iron to Norway; the Fleur d'Epine of this town, a good ship, and a sure, and he her mate; and as proud as might be, and with a little blest Mary in lead round his throat.

"She was to be back in port in eight months, bringing timber. Eight months—that brought Easter time.

"But she never came. Never, never, never, you know.

"I sat here watching them come and go, and my child sickened and died, and the summer passed, and the autumn, and all the while I looked—looked —looked; for the brigs are all much alike; only his I always saw as soon as she hove in sight be- cause he tied a hank of flax to her mizen mast; and when he was home safe and sound I spun the hank into hose for him; that was a fancy of his, and for eleven voyages, one on another, he had never missed to tie the flax nor I to spin the hose.

"But the hank of flax I never saw this time; nor the brave brig; nor my good man with his sunny blue eyes.

"Only one day in winter, when the great blocks

of ice were smashing hither and thither, a coaster came in and brought tidings of how off in the Danish waters they had come on a waterlogged brig, and had boarded her, and had found her empty, and her hull riven in two, and her crew all drowned and dead beyond any manner of doubt. And on her stern there was her name painted white, the Fleur d'Epine, of Brussels, as plain as name could be; and that was all we ever knew—what evil had struck her, or how they had perished, nobody ever told.

"Only the coaster brought that bit of beam away, with the Fleur d'Epine writ clear upon it.

"But you see I never *know* my man is dead.

"Any day—who can say?—any of those ships may bring him aboard of her, and he may leap out on the wharf there, and come running up the stairs as he used to do, and cry, in his merry voice, 'Annémie, Annémie, here is more flax to spin, here is more hose to weave!' For that was always his homeward word; no matter whether he had had fair weather or foul, he always knotted the flax to his mast-head.

"So you see, dear, I could not leave here. For what if he came and found me away. He would say it was an odd fashion of mourning for him.

"And I could not do without the window, you know. I can watch all the brigs come in; and I can smell the shipping smell that I have loved all the days of my life; and I can see the lads heaving, and climbing, and furling, and mending their bits of canvas, and hauling their flags up and down.

"And then who can say?—the sea never took him, I think—I think I shall hear his voice before I die.

"For they do say that God is good."

Bébée sweeping very noiselessly, listened, and her eyes grew wistful and wondering. She had heard the story a thousand times; always in different words, but always the same little tale, and she knew how old Annémie was deaf to all the bells that tolled the time, and blind to all the whiteness of her hair, and all the wrinkles of her face, and only thought of her sea-slain lover as he had been in the days of her youth.

But this afternoon the familiar history had a

new patheticness for her, and as the old soul put aside with her palsied hand the square of canvas that screened the casement, and looked out, with her old dim sad eyes strained in the longing that God never answered, Bébée felt a strange chill at her own heart, and wondered to herself:—

"What can it be to care for another creature like that! It must be so terrible, and yet it must be beautiful too—does everyone suffer like that!"

She did not speak at all as she finished sweeping the bricks, and went downstairs for a metal cruche full of water, and set over a little charcoal on the stove the old woman's brass soup kettle with her supper of stewing cabbage.

Annémie did not hear or notice; she was still looking out of the hole in the wall on to the masts and the sails and the water.

It was twilight.

From the barges and brigs there came the smell of the sea. The sailors were shouting to each other. The craft were crowded close, and lost in the growing darkness. On the other side of the canal the belfries were ringing for vespers.

"Eleven voyages one and another, and he never forgot to tie the flax to the mast," Annémie murmured, with her old wrinkled face leaning out into the grey air. "It used to fly there—one could see it coming up half-a-mile off,—just a pale yellow flake on the wind, like a tress of my hair, he would say. No, no, I could not go away; he may come to-night, to-morrow, any time; he is not drowned, not my man; he was all I had, and God is good, they say."

Bébée listened and looked; then kissed the old shaking hand, and took up the lace patterns and went softly out of the room without speaking.

When old Annémie watched at the window it was useless to seek for any word or sign of her; people said that she had never been quite right in her brain since that fatal winter noon sixty years before, when the coaster had brought into port the broken beam of the good brig Fleur d'Epine.

Bébée did not know about that, nor heed whether her wits were right or not.

She had known the old creature in the lace-room where Annémie pricked out designs, and she had conceived a great regard and sorrow for her; and when Annémie had become too ailing and aged to go herself any longer to the lacemaker's place, Bébée had begged leave for her to have the patterns at home, and had carried them to and fro for her for the last three or four years, doing many other little useful services for the lone old soul as well—services which Annémie hardly perceived, she had grown so used to them, and her feeble intelligence was so sunk in the one absorbing idea that she must watch all the days through and all the years through for the coming of the dead man and the lost brig.

Bébée put the lace patterns in her basket, and trotted home, her sabots clattering on the stones.

"What it must be to care for anyone like that!" she thought, and, by some vague association of thought that she could not have pursued, she lifted the leaves and looked at the moss rosebud.

It was quite dead.

————

## CHAPTER VI.

As she got clear of the city and out on her country road, a shadow fell across her in the evening light.

"Have you had a good day, little one?" asked a voice, that made her stop with a curious vague expectancy and pleasure.

"It is you!" she said, with a little cry, as she saw her friend of the silk stockings leaning on a gate midway in the green and solitary road that leads to Laeken.

"Yes, it is I," he answered, as he joined her. "Have you forgiven me, Bébée?"

She looked at him with frank, appealing eyes, like those of a child in fault.

"Oh, I did not sleep all night," she said, simply. "I thought I had been rude and ungrateful, and I could not be sure I had done right, though to have done otherwise would certainly have been wrong."

He laughed.

"Well, that is a clearer deduction than is to be drawn from most moral uncertainties. Do not think twice about the matter, my dear. I have not, I assure you."

"No!"

She was a little disappointed. It seemed such an immense thing to her; and she had lain awake all the night, turning it about in her little brain, and appealing vainly for help in it to the sixteen sleep-angels.

"No, indeed. And where are you going so fast, as if those wooden shoes of yours were sandals of Mercury?"

"Mercury—is that a shoemaker?"

"No, my dear. He did a terrible bit of cobbling once, when he made Woman. But he did not shoe her feet with swiftness that I know of; she only runs away to be run after, and if you do not pursue her, she comes back—always."

Bébée did not understand at all.

"I thought God made women?" she said, a little awe-stricken.

"You call it God. People three thousand years ago called it Mercury or Hermes. Both mean the same thing,—mere words to designate an unknown quality. Where are you going? Does your home lie here?"

"Yes, onward, quite far onward," said Bébée, wondering that he had forgotten all she had told him the day before about her hut, her garden, and her neighbours. "You did not come and finish your picture to day, why was that? I had a rosebud for you, but it is dead now."

"I went to Anvers. You looked for me a little, then?"

"Oh, all day long. For I was so afraid I had been ungrateful."

"That is very pretty of you. Women are never grateful, my dear, except when they are very ill treated. Mercury, whom we were talking of, gave them, amongst other gifts, a dog's heart."

Bébée felt bewildered; she did not reason about it, but the idle, shallow, cynical tone pained her by its levity and its unlikeness to the sweet, still, grey summer evening.

"Why are you in such a hurry?" he pursued. "The night is cool, and it is only seven o'clock. I will walk part of the way with you."

"I am in a hurry because I have Annémie's patterns to do," said Bébée, glad that he spoke of a thing that she knew how to answer. "You see, Annémie's hand shakes and her eyes are dim, and she pricks the pattern all awry and never perceives it; it would break her heart if one showed her so, but the Baes would not take them as they are; they are of no use at all. So I prick them out myself on fresh paper, and the Baes thinks it is all her doing, and pays her the same money, and she is quite content. And as I carry the patterns to and fro for her, because she cannot walk, it is easy to cheat her like that; and it is no harm to cheat *so*, you know."

He was silent.

"You are a good little girl, Bébée, I can see," he said at last, with a graver sound in his voice. "And who is this Annémie for whom you do so much—an old woman, I suppose?"

"Oh, yes, quite old; incredibly old. Her man

was drowned at sea sixty years ago, and she watches for his brig still, night and morning."

"The dog's heart. No doubt he beat her, and had a wife in fifty other ports."

"Oh, no," said Bébée, with a little cry, as though the word against the dead man hurt her. "She has told me so much of him. He was as good as good could be, and loved her so, and between the voyages they were so happy. Surely that must have been; sixty years now, and she is so sorry still, and still will not believe that he was drowned."

He looked down on her with a smile that had a certain pity in it.

"Well, yes; there are women like that, I believe. But be very sure, my dear, he beat her. Of the two, one always holds the whip and uses it,—the other crouches."

"I do not understand," said Bébée.

"No—but you will."

"I will?—when?"

He smiled again.

"Oh—to-morrow perhaps, or next year — or when Fate fancies.

"Or rather — when I choose," he thought to himself, and let his eyes rest with a certain pleasure on the little feet, that went beside him in the grass, and the pretty neck that showed ever and again, as the frills of her linen bodice were blown back by the wind, and her own quick motion.

Bébée looked also up at him; he was very handsome, or looked so to her, after the broad blunt characterless faces of the Brabantois around her. He walked with an easy grace, he was clad in picture-like velvets, he had a beautiful poetic head, and eyes like deep brown waters, and a face like one of Jordaens' or Rembrandt's cavaliers in the galleries where she used to steal in of a Sunday, and look up at the paintings, and dream of what that world could be in which those people had lived.

"*You* are of the people of Rubes' country, are you not?" she asked him.

"Of what country, my dear?"

"Of the people that live in the gold frames,"

said Bébée, quite seriously. "In the galleries, you
know—I know a charwoman that scrubs the floors
of the Arenenberg, and she lets me in sometimes
to look—and you are just like those great gentle-
men in the gold frames, only you have not a hawk
and a sword, and they always have. I used to
wonder where they came from, for they are not
like any of us one bit, and the charwoman—she is
Lisa Dredel, and lives in the street of the Pot
d'Etain—always said, 'Dear heart, they all belong
to Rubes' land—we never see their like now-a-days.'
But *you* must come out of Rubes' land; at least, I
think so, do you not?"

He caught her meaning; he knew that Rubes
was the homely abbreviation of Rubens, that all the
Netherlanders used, and he guessed the idea that
was reality to this little lonely fanciful mind.

"Perhaps I do," he answered her with a smile,
for it was not worth his while to disabuse her
thoughts of any imagination that glorified him to
her. "Do you not want to see Rubes' world, little
one? To see the gold and the grandeur, and the
glitter of it all?—never to toil or get tired?—always

to move in a pageant?—always to live like the
hawks in the paintings you talk of, with silver
bells hung round you, and a hood all sewn with
pearls?"

"No," said Bébée, simply. "I should like to
see it—just to see it, as one looks through a grating
into the king's grape-houses here. But I should
not like to live in it. I love my hut, and the
starling, and the chickens, and what would the
garden do without me?—and the children, and the
old Annémie? I could not anyhow, anywhere be
any happier than I am. There is only one thing I
wish."

"And what is that?"

"To know something. Not to be so ignorant;
just look—I can read a little, it is true, my hours,
and the letters, and when Krebs brings in a newspaper I can read a little of it—not much. I know
French well, because Antoine was French himself,
and never did talk Flemish to me; and they, being
Flemish, cannot, of course, read the newspapers at
all, and so think it very wonderful indeed in me.
But what I want is to know things, to know all

about what *was* before ever I was living. Ste.
Gudule now—they say it was built hundreds of
years before; and Rubes again—they say he was a
painter-king in Antwerpen before the oldest
woman like Annémie ever began to count time. I
am sure books tell you all those things, because I
see the students coming and going with them; and
when I saw once the millions of books in the Rue
de la Musée, I asked the keeper what use they were
for, and he said, 'to make men wise, my dear.' But
Bac the cobbler, who was with me,— it was a fête
day—Bac, *he* said, 'Do not you believe that, Bébée;
they only muddle folk's brains; for one book tells
them one thing, and another book another, and so
on, till they are dazed with all the contrary lying;
and if you see a bookish man, be sure you see a
very poor creature who could not hoe a patch, or
kill a pig, or stitch an upperleather, were it ever
so.' But I do not believe that Bac said right. Did
he?"

"I am not sure. On the whole, I think it is the
truest remark on literature I have ever heard, and
one that shows great judgment in Bac. Well?"

"Well—sometimes, you know," said Bébée, not understanding his answer, but pursuing her thoughts confidentially; "sometimes I talk like this to the neighbours, and they laugh at me. Because Mère Krebs says that when one knows how to spin and sweep and make bread and say one's prayers and milk a goat or a cow, it is all a woman wants to know this side of heaven. But for me, I cannot help it—when I look at those windows in the cathedral, or at those beautiful twisted little spires that are all over our Hôtel de Ville, I want to know who the men were that made them—what they did and thought—how they looked and spoke—how they learned to shape stone into leaves and grasses like that—how they could imagine all those angel faces on the glass. When I go alone in the quite early morning or at night when it is still—sometimes in winter I have to stay till it is dark over the lace—I hear their feet come after me, and they whisper to me close, 'Look what beautiful things we have done, Bébée, and you all forget us quite. We did what never will die, but our names are as dead as the stones.' And then I am so sorry for

them and ashamed. And I want to know more.
Can you tell me?"

He looked at her earnestly; her eyes were
shining, her cheeks were warm, her little mouth was
tremulous with eagerness.

"Did anyone ever speak to you in that way?"
he asked her.

"No," she answered him. "It comes into my
head of itself. Sometimes I think the cathedral
angels put it there. For the angels must be tired,
you know; always pointing to God and always
seeing men turn away. I used to tell Antoine
sometimes. But he used to shake his head and say
that it was no use thinking; most likely Ste. Gudule
and St. Michael had set the church down in the
night all ready made, why not? God made the
trees, and they were more wonderful, he thought,
for his part. And so perhaps they are, but that is
no answer. And I do *want* to know. I want some
one who will tell me, — and if you come out of
Rubes' country as I think, no doubt you know everything, or remember it?"

He smiled.

"The free pass to Rubes' country lies in books, pretty one. Shall I give you some?—nay, lend them, I mean, since giving you are too wilful to hear of without offence. You can read, you said?"

Bébée's eyes glowed as they lifted themselves to his.

"I can read—not very fast, but that would come with doing it more and more, I think, just as spinning does—one knots the thread and breaks it a million times before one learns to spin as fine as cobwebs. I have read the stories of S. Anne, and of S. Catherine, and of S. Lieven fifty times, but they are all the books that Father Francis has; and no one else has any amongst us."

"Very well. You shall have books of mine. Easy ones first; and then those that are more serious. But what time will you have? You do so much; you are like a little golden bee."

Bébée laughed happily.

"Oh! give me the books and I will find the time. It is light so early now. That gives one so many hours. In winter one has so few, one must lie in bed, because to buy a candle you know one cannot

afford except, of course, a taper now and then, as
one's duty is, for Our Lady or for the dead.  And
will you really, really, lend me books?"

"Really—I will.  Yes.  I will bring you one to
the Grande Place to-morrow, or meet you on your
road here with it.  Do you know what poetry is,
Bébée?"

"No."

"But your flowers talk to you?"

"Ah! always.  But then no one else hears them
ever but me; and so no one else ever believes."

"Well—poets are folks who hear the flowers
talk as you do, and the trees, and the seas, and the
beasts, and even the stones; but no one else ever
hears these things, and so, when the poets write
them out, the rest of the world say, 'That is very
fine, no doubt, but only good for dreamers; it will
bake no bread.'  I will give you some poetry—for
I think you care more about dreams than about
bread."

"I do not know," said Bébée; and she did not
know, for her dreams, like her youth, and her innocence, and her simplicity, and her strength, were

all unconscious of themselves, as such things must be to be pure and true at all.

Bébée had grown up straight, and clean, and fragrant, and joyous as one of her own carnations; but she knew herself no more than the carnation knows its colour and its root.

"No, you do not know," said he, with a sort of pity, and thought within himself—was it worth while to let her know?

If she did not know, these vague aspirations and imaginations would drop off from her with the years of her early youth, as the lime-flowers drop downwards with the summer heats. She would forget them. They would linger a little in her heart, and, perhaps, always wake at some sunset hour or some angelus chime, but not to trouble her. Only to make her cradle-song a little sadder and softer than most women's was. Unfed, they would sink away and bear no blossom. She would grow into a simple, hardy, hard-working, God-fearing Flemish woman like the rest. She would marry, no doubt, sometime, and rear her children honestly and well; and sit in the market stall every day, and

spin and sew, and dig and wash, and sweep, and
brave bad weather, and be content with poor food
to the end of her harmless and laborious days—
poor little Bébée.

He saw her so clearly as she would be—if he
let her alone.

A little taller, a little broader, a little browner,
less soft of skin, less flower-like in face; having
learned to think only as her neighbours thought of
price of wood and cost of bread; labouring cheerily
but hardly from daybreak to nightfall to fill hungry
mouths; forgetting all things except the little curly
heads clustered round her soup-pot, and the year-
old lips sucking at her breast.

A blameless life, an eventless life, a life as clear
as the dewdrop, and as colourless; a life opening,
passing, ending in the little green wooded lane, by
the bit of water where the swans made their nests
under the willows; a life like the life of millions, a
little purer, a little brighter, a little more tender,
perhaps, than those lives usually are, but otherwise
as like them as one ear of barley is like another as
it rises from the soil, and blows in the wind, and

turns brown in the strong summer sun, and then goes down to the sod again under the sickle.

He saw her just as she would be—if he let her alone.

But should he leave her alone?

He cared nothing; only her eyes had such a pretty, frank, innocent look like a bird's in them, and she had been so brave and bold with him about those silken stockings; and this little ignorant, dreamful mind of hers was so like a blush rosebud, which looks so close shut, and so sweet smelling, and so tempting fold within fold, that a child will pull it open, forgetful that he will spoil it for ever, and for ever prevent it from being a full-grown rose, and that he will let the dust, and the sun, and the bee into its tender bosom. Now men are true children, and women are their rosebuds.

Thinking only of keeping well with this strange and beautiful wayfarer from that unknown paradise of Rubes' country, she opened the leaves of her basket.

"I took a bouquet for you to-day, but it is dead.

8*

Look—to-morrow, if you will be there, you shall have the best in all the garden."

"You wish to see me again then?" he asked her. Bébée looked at him with troubled eyes, but with a sweet frank faith that had no hesitation in it.

"Yes! you are not like anything I ever knew, and if you will only help me to learn a little I shall be so thankful: sometimes I think I am not stupid, only ignorant,—but I cannot be sure unless I try."

He smiled; he was listlessly amused; the day before he had tempted the child merely because she was pretty, and to tempt her in that way seemed the natural course of things, but now there was something in her that touched him differently; the end would be the same, but he would change the means.

The sun had set. There was a low, dull red glow still on the far edge of the plains—that was all. In the distant cottages little lights were twinkling. The path grew dark.

"I will go away and let her alone," he thought. "Poor little soul! it would give itself lavishly, it would never be bought. I will let it alone; the mind will go to sleep, and the body will keep healthy and strong and pure, as people call it. It would be a pity to play with both a day, and then throw them away as a boy throws a dead sparrow. She is a little clod of earth that has field-flowers growing in it. I will let her alone; the flowers under the plough in due course will die, and she will be content amongst the other clods;— if I let her alone."

At that moment there went across the dark fields, against the dusky red sky, a young man with a pile of brushwood on his back, and a hatchet in his hand.

"You are late, Bébée," he called to her in Flemish, and scowled at the stranger by her side.

"A good-looking lad—who is it?" said her companion.

"That is Jeannot, the son of old Sophie," she answered him. "He is so good—oh, so good, you cannot think; he keeps his mother and three little sisters, and works so very, very hard in the forest, and yet he often finds time to dig my garden for me, and he chops all my wood in winter."

They had come to where the road goes up by the king's summer-palace.

They were under great hanging beeches and limes. There was a high grey wall, and over it the blossoming fruit-boughs hung. In a ditch full of long grass little kids bleated by their mothers.

Away on the left went the green fields of colza, and beetroot, and trefoil, with big forest trees here and there in their midst, and, against the blue low line of the far horizon, red mill-sails and grey church spires; dreamy plaintive bells far away somewhere were ringing the sad Flemish carillon.

He paused and looked at her.

"I must bid you good-night, Bébée—you are near your home now."

She paused too and looked at him.

"But I shall see you to-morrow?"

There was the wistful, eager, anxious unconsciousness of appeal as when, the night before, she had asked him if he were angry.

He hesitated a moment. If he said No, and went away out of the city wherever his listless and changeful whim called him, he knew how it would be with her; he knew what her life would be as surely as he knew the peach would come out of the peachflower rosy on the wall there; life in the little hut; among the neighbours; sleepy and safe and soulless;—if he let her alone.

If he stayed and saw her on the morrow he knew, too, the end as surely as he knew that the branch of white pear-blossom, which in care-lessness he had knocked down with a stone on the grass yonder, would fade in the night and would never bring forth its sweet, simple fruit in the sunshine.

To leave the peachflower to come to maturity and be plucked by a peasant—or to pull down the pear-blossom and rifle the buds?

Carelessly and languidly he balanced the ques-tion with himself, whilst Bébée, forgetful of the lace

patterns and the flight of the hours, stood looking
at him with anxious and pleading eyes, thinking
only—was he angry again, or would he really bring
her the books and make her wise, and let her know
the stories of the past?

"Shall I see you to-morrow?" she said wistfully.

Should she?—if he left the peach-blossom safe
on the wall, Jeannot the woodcutter would come
by-and-by and gather the fruit.

If he left the clod of earth in its pasture with
all its daisies untouched, this black-browed young
peasant would cut it round with his hatchet and
carry it to his wicker cage, that the homely brown
lark of his love might sing to it some stupid wood-
note under a cottage eave.

The sight of the strong young forester going
over the darkened fields against the dull red skies
was as a feather that suffices to sway to one side a
balance that hangs on a hair.

He had been inclined to leave her alone, when
he saw in his fancy the clean, simple, mindless,
honest life that her fanciful girlhood would settle

down into as time should go on. But when in the figure of the woodman there was painted visibly on the dusky sky that end for her which he had fore-seen, he was not indifferent to it; he resented it; he was stirred to a vague desire to render it impossible.

If Jeannot had not gone by across the fields, he would have left her and let her alone from that night thenceforwards; as it was—

"Good-night, Bébée," he said to her. "To-morrow I will finish the Broodhuis and bring you your first book. Do not dream too much, or you will prick your lace patterns all awry. Good-night, pretty one."

Then he turned and went back through the green dim lanes to the city.

Bébée stood a moment looking after him, with a happy smile; then she picked up the fallen pear-bough, and ran home as fast as her feet would take her.

That night she worked very late watering her flowers, and trimming them, and then ironing out a little clean white cap for the morrow; and then sitting down under the open lattice to prick out all old Annémie's designs by the strong light of the full moon that flooded her hut with its radiance.

But she sang all the time she worked, and the gay, pretty, wordless songs floated across the water and across the fields, and woke some old people in their beds as they lay with their windows open, and they turned and crossed themselves, and said, "Dear heart!—this is the Eve of the Ascension, and the angels are so near we hear them."

But it was no angel; only the thing that is nearer heaven than anything else—a little human heart that is happy and innocent.

Bébée had only one sorrow that night. The pear-blossoms were all dead—and no care could call them back even for an hour's blooming.

"He did not think when he struck them down," she said to herself regretfully.

## CHAPTER VII.

"CAN I do any work for you, Bébée?" said black Jeannot in the daybreak, pushing her gate open timidly with one hand.

"There is none to do, Jeannot. They want so little in this time of the year—the flowers," said she, lifting her head from the sweet peas she was tying up to their sticks.

The woodman did not answer; he leaned over the half-open wicket, and swayed it backwards and forwards under his bare arm. He was a good, harmless, gentle fellow, swarthy as charcoal and simple as a child, and quite ignorant; having spent all his days in the great Soignies forests, making faggots when he was a little lad, and hewing down trees or burning charcoal as he grew to manhood.

"Who was that seigneur with you last night,

Bébée?" he asked, after a long silence, watching her as she moved.

Bébée's eyes grew very soft, but they looked up frankly.

"I am not sure. I think he is a painter—a great painter-prince I mean—as Rubes was in Antwerpen; he wanted roses the night before last in the Cathedral."

"But he was walking with you?"

"He was in the lane as I came home last night —yes."

"What does he give you for your roses?"

"Oh—he pays me well. How is your mother this day, Jeannot?"

"You do not like to talk of him?"

"Why should you want to talk of him?—he is nothing to you."

"Did you really see him only two days ago, Bébée?"

"Oh, Jeannot!—did I ever tell a falsehood? —you would not say that to one of your little sisters."

The forester swayed the gate to and fro drearily under his folded arms.

Bébée, not regarding him, cut her flowers, and filled her baskets, and did her other work, and set a ladder against the hut and climbed on its low roof to seek for eggs, the hens having strange tastes sometimes for the rushes and lichens of its thatch. She found two eggs, which she promised herself to take to Annémie, and looking round as she sat on the edge of the roof, with one foot on the highest rung of the ladder, saw that Jeannot was still at the gate.

"You will be late in the forest, Jeannot," she cried to him. "It is such a long, long way in and out. Why do you look so sulky? and you are kicking the wicket to pieces."

"I do not like you to talk with strangers," said Jeannot, sullenly and sadly.

Bébée laughed as she sat on the edge of the thatch, and looked at the shining grey skies of the early day, and the dew-wet garden, and the green fields beyond, with happy eyes that made the familiar scene transfigured to her.

"Oh, Jeannot, what nonsense! As if I do not talk to a million strangers every summer; as if I could ever sell a flower if I did not! You are cross this morning—that is what it is."

"Do you know the man's name?" said Jeannot, suddenly.

Bébée felt her cheeks grow warm as with some noonday heat of sunshine. She thought it was with anger against blundering Jeannot's curiosity.

"No! and what would his name be to us, if I did know it! I cannot ask people's names because they buy my roses."

"As if it were only roses!——"

There was the length of the garden between them, and Bébée did not hear as she sat on the edge of her roof with that light dreamful enjoyment of air and sky and coolness, and all the beauty of the dawning day, which the sweet vague sense of a personal happiness will bring with it to the dullest and the coldest.

"You are cross, Jeannot, that is what it is," she said, after a while. "You should not be cross; you are too big and strong and good. Go in and get my bowl of bread and milk for me, and hand it to me up here. It is so pleasant. It is as nice as being perched on an apple-tree."

Jeannot went in obediently and handed up her breakfast to her, looking at her with shy, worshipping eyes. But his face was overcast, and he sighed heavily as he took up his hatchet and turned away; for he was the sole support of his mother and sisters, and if he did not do his work in Soignies they would starve at home.

"You will be seeing that stranger again?" he asked her.

"Yes!" she answered, with a glad triumph in her eyes; not thinking at all of him as she spoke. "You ought to go, Jeannot, now; you are so late. I will come and see your mother to-morrow. And do not be cross, you dear big Jeannot. Days are too short to snip them up into little bits by bad temper; it is only a stupid sheep-shearer that spoils the fleece by snapping at it sharp and hard—that is what Father Francis says."

Bébée having delivered her little piece of wisdom, broke her bread into her milk and ate it, lifting her face to the fresh wind and tossing crumbs to the wheeling swallows, and watching the rose-bushes nod and toss below in the breeze, and thinking vaguely how happy a thing it was to live.

Jeannot looked up at her, then went on his slow sad way through the wet lavender shrubs and the opening buds of the lilies.

"You will only think of that stranger, Bébée, never of any of us—never again," he said; and wearily opened the little gate and went through it, and down the daybreak stillness of the lane. It was a foolish thing to say; but when were lovers ever wise?

Bébée did not heed; she did not understand herself or him; she only knew that she was happy; when one knows that, one does not want to seek much farther.

She sat on the thatch and took her bread and milk in the grey clear air, with the swallows circling above her head, and one or two of them even resting a second on the edge of the bowl to peck at the food from the big wooden spoon; they had known her all the sixteen summers of her life, and

were her playfellows, only they would never tell
her anything of what they saw in winter over the
seas. That was her only quarrel with them. Swallows do not tell their secrets. They have the weird
of Procne on them all.

The Sun came and touched the lichens of the
roof into gold.

Bébée smiled at it gaily as it rose above the
tops of the trees, and shone on all the little villages
scattered over the plains.

"Ah, dear Sun!" she cried to it. "I am going
to be wise. I am going into great Rubes' country.
I am going to hear of the Past and the Future. I
am going to listen to what the Poets say. The
swallows never would tell me anything; but now I
shall know as much as they know. Are you not
glad for me, oh Sun?"

The Sun came over the trees, and heard and
said nothing. If he had answered at all he must
have said:—

"The only time when a human soul is either
wise or happy, is in that one single moment when
the hour of my own shining or of the moon's beam-

ing seems to that single soul, to be past and present and future, to be at once the creation and the end of all things. Faust knew that; so will you."

But the Sun shone on and held his peace. He sees all things ripen and fall. He can wait. He knows the end. It is always the same.

He brings the fruit out of the peach-flower, and rounds it and touches it into ruddiest rose and softest gold; but the sun knows well that the peach must drop—whether into the basket to be eaten by kings, or on to the turf to be eaten by ants. What matter which very much after all?

The Sun is not a cynic; he is only wise because he is Life and he is Death, the creator and the corrupter of all things.

———————

## CHAPTER VIIL

But Bébée, who only saw in the Sun the sign of daily work, the brightness of the face of the world, the friend of the flowers, the harvest-man of the poor, the playmate of the birds and butterflies, the kindly light that the waking birds and the ringing carillon welcomed—Bébée, who was not at all afraid of him, smiled at his rays and saw in them only fairest promise of a cloudless midsummer day as she gave her last crumb to the swallows, dropped down off the thatch, and busied herself in making bread, that Mère Krebs would bake for her, until it was time to cut her flowers and go down into the town.

When her loaves were made and she had run over with them to the mill-house and back again, she attired herself with more heed than usual, and ran to look at her own face in the mirror of the deep well-water—other glass she had none.

9*

She was used to hear herself called pretty; but she had never thought about it at all till now. The people loved her; she had always believed that they had only said it as a sort of kindness, as they said, "God keep you." But now——

"He told me I was like a flower," she thought to herself, and hung over the well to see. She did not know very well what he had meant; but the sentence stirred in her heart as a little bird under tremulous leaves.

She waited ten minutes full, leaning and looking down, while her eyes, that were like the blue iris, smiled back to her from the brown depths below. Then she went and kneeled down before the old shrine in the wall of the garden.

"Dear and holy Mother of Jesus, I do thank you that you made me a little good to look at," she said, softly. "Keep me as you keep the flowers, and let my face be always fair, because it is a pleasure to *be* a pleasure. Ah, dear Mother, I say it so badly, and it sounds so vain, I know. But I do not think you will be angry, will you? And I am going to try to be wise."

TWO LITTLE WOODEN SHOES.

Then she murmured an ave or two, to be in form as it were, and then rose and ran along the lanes with her baskets, and brushed the dew lightly over her bare feet, and sang a little Flemish song for very joyousness, as the birds sing in the apple-bough.

She got the money for Annémie and took it to her with fresh patterns to prick, and the new-laid eggs.

"I wonder what he meant by a dog's heart?" she thought to herself, as she left the old woman sitting by the hole in the roof pricking out the parchment in all faith that she earned her money, and looking every now and then through the forests of masts for the brig with the hank of flax flying; the brig that had foundered sixty long years before in the northern seas, and in the days of her youth.

"What is the dog's heart?" thought Bébée; she had seen a dog she knew—a dog who all his life long had dragged heavy loads under brutal stripes along the streets of Brussels—stretch himself on the grave of his taskmaster and refuse to eat, and persist in lying there until he died, though he had no

memory except of stripes, and no tie to the dead
except pain and sorrow; was it a heart like this that
he meant?

"Was her sailor, indeed, so good to her?" she
asked an old gossip of Annémie's, as she went down
the stairs.

The old soul stopped to think with difficulty of
such a far off time, and resting her brass flagon of
milk on the steep step,

"Eh, no; not that I ever saw," she answered at
length. "He was fond of her—very fond; but he
was a wilful one, and he beat her sometimes when
he got tired of being on land. But women must
not mind that, you know, my dear, if only a man's
heart is right. Things fret them, and then they
belabour what they love best; it is a way they
have."

"But she speaks of him as of an angel nearly?"
said Bébée bewildered.

The old woman took up her flagon, with a smile
flitting across her wintry face.

"Ay, dear; when the frost kills your brave rosebush, root and bud, do you think of the thorns that

pricked you, or only of the fair, sweet-smelling things that flowered all your summer?"

Bébée went away thoughtfully out of the old crazy water-washed house by the quay; and into the square to her familiar place: life seemed growing very strange and intricate and knotted about her, like the threads of lace that a bad fairy has entangled in the night.

———

## CHAPTER IX.

HER stranger from Rubes' Land was a great
man in a certain world. He had become great
when young, which is perhaps a misfortune. It in-
disposes men to be great at their maturity. He was
famous at twenty, by a picture hectic in colour,
perfect in drawing, that made Paris at his feet. He
became more famous by verses, by plays, by political
follies, and by social successes. He was faithful,
however, to his first love in art. He was a great
painter, and year by year proved afresh the cunning
of his hand. Purists said his pictures had no soul
in them. It was not wonderful if they had none.
He always painted soulless vice; indeed, he saw
very little else.

One year he had some political trouble. He
wrote a witty pamphlet that hurt where it was peril-
ous to aim. He laughed and crossed the border,
riding into the green Ardennes one sunny evening.
He had a name of some power and sufficient

wealth; he did not fear long exile. Meanwhile he told himself he would go and look at Scheffer's Gretchen.

The King of Thule is better; but people talk most of the Gretchen. He had never seen either.

He went in leisurely, travelling up the bright Meuse river, and across the monotony of the plains, then green with wheat a foot high, and musical with the many bells of the Easter kermesses in the quaint old-world villages.

There was something so novel, so sleepy, so harmless, so mediæval, in the Flemish life, that it soothed him. He had been swimming all his life in salt sea-fed rapids; this sluggish, dull canal-water, mirroring between its rushes a life that had scarcely changed for centuries, had a charm for him.

He stayed awhile in Antwerpen. The town is ugly and beautiful; it is like a dull quaint grès de Flandre jug, that has precious stones set inside its rim. It is a burgher ledger of bales and barrels, of sale and barter, of loss and gain; but in the heart of it there are illuminated leaves of missal vellum,

all gold and colour, and monkish story and heroic
ballad, that could only have been executed in the
days when Art was a religion.

He gazed himself into a homage of Rubens,
whom before he had slighted, never having known;
(for, unless you have seen Antwerp, it is as absurd
to say that you have seen Rubens as it is to think
that you have seen Murillo out of Seville, or Raf-
faelle out of Rome;) and he studied the Gretchen
carefully, delicately, sympathetically, for he loved
Scheffer; but though he tried, he failed to care for
her.

"She is only a peasant; she is not a poem," he
said to himself; "I will paint a Gretchen for the
Salon of next year."

But it was hard for him to pourtray a Gretchen.
All his pictures were Phryne—Phryne in triumph,
in ruin, in a palace, in a poorhouse, on a bed of
roses, on a hospital mattress; Phryne laughing with
a belt of jewels about her supple waist; Phryne
lying with the stones of the dead-house under her
naked limbs—but always Phryne. Phryne, who
living had death in her smile; Phryne, who lifeless

had blank despair on her face; Phryne, a thing that lived furiously every second of her days, but Phryne a thing that once being dead was carrion that never could live again.

Phryne has many painters in this school, as many as Catherine and Cecilia had in the schools of the Renaissance, and he was chief amidst them.

How could he paint Gretchen if the pure Scheffer missed? Not even if, like the artist monks of old, he steeped his brushes all Lent through in holy water.

And in holy water he did not believe.

One evening, having left Antwerpen ringing its innumerable bells over the grave of its dead Art, he leaned out of the casement of an absent friend's old palace in the Brabant street that is named after Mary of Burgundy; an old casement crusted with quaint carvings, and gilded round in Spanish fashion, with many gargoyles and griffins, and illegible scutcheons.

Leaning there, wondering with himself whether he would wait awhile and paint quietly in this dim

street, haunted with the shades of Memling and
Maes, and Otto Veneris and Philip de Champagne,
or whether he would go into the East and seek new
types, and lie under the red Egyptian heavens and
create a true Cleopatra which no man has ever
done yet—a young Cleopatra, ankle deep in roses
and fresh from Cæsar's kisses—leaning there, he
saw a little peasant go by below, with two little
white feet in two wooden shoes, and a face that
had the pure and simple radiance of a flower.

"There is my Gretchen," he thought to himself,
and went down and followed her into the Cathedral.
If he could get what was in her face, he would get
what Scheffer could not.

A little later walking by her in the green lanes
he meditated, "It is the face of Gretchen, but not
the soul—the Red Mouse has never passed this
child's lips. Nevertheless——"

"Nevertheless——" he said to himself, and
smiled.

For he, the painter all his life long of Phryne
living and of Phryne dead, believed that every

daughter of Eve either vomits the Red Mouse or swallows it.

It makes so little difference which,—either way the Red Mouse has been there.

And yet, strolling there in the dusky red of the evening towards this little rush-covered hut, he forgot the Red Mouse, and began vaguely to see that there are creatures of his mother's sex from whom the beast of the Brocken slinks away.

But he still said to himself, "Nevertheless."

"Nevertheless,"—for he knew well that when the steel cuts the silk, when the hound hunts the fawn, when the snake woos the bird, when the king covets the vineyard, there is only one end possible at any time. It is the strong against the weak, the fierce against the feeble, the subtle against the simple, the master against the slave; there is no equality in the contest and no justice—it is merely inevitable, and the issue of it is written.

## CHAPTER X.

THE next day she had her promised book hidden under the vine-leaves of her empty basket as she went homeward, and though she had not seen him very long or spoken to him very much, she was happy.

The golden gates of knowledge had just opened to her; she saw a faint, far-off glimpse of the Hesperides gardens within: of the dragon she had never heard, and had no fear.

"Might I know your name?" she had asked him wistfully, as she had given him the rosebud, and taken the volume in return that day.

"They call me Flamen."

"It is your name?"

"Yes, for the world. You must call me Victor, as other women do. Why do you want my name?"

"Jeannot asked it of me."

"Oh, Jeannot asked it, did he?"

"Yes, besides," said Bébée, with her eyes very soft and very serious, and her happy voice hushed, "besides I want to pray for you of course, every day, and if I do not know your name, how can I make Our Lady rightly understand? The flowers know you without a name, but she might not, because so very many are always beseeching her, and you see she has all the world to look after."

He had looked at her with a curious look, and had bade her farewell, and let her go home alone that night.

Her work was quickly done, and by the light of the moon she spread her book on her lap in the porch of the hut and began her new delight.

The children had come and pulled at her skirts and begged her to play. But Bébée had shaken her head.

"I am going to learn to be very wise, dear," she told them; "I shall not have time to dance or to play."

"But people are not merry when they are wise, Bébée," said Franz, the biggest boy.

"Perhaps not," said Bébée; "but one cannot be everything, you know, Franz."

"But surely, you would rather be merry than anything else?"

"I think there is something better, Franz. I am not sure; I want to find out; I will tell you when I know."

"Who has put that into your head, Bébée?"

"The angels in the Cathedral," she told them, and the children were awed and left her, and went away to play blindman's-buff by themselves on the grass by the swan's water.

"But for all that the angels have said it," said Franz to his sisters, "I cannot see what good it will be to her to be wise, if she will not care any longer afterwards for almond ginger-bread, and currant cake."

It was the little tale of "Paul and Virginia" that he had given her to begin her studies with; but it was a grand copy, full of beautiful drawings nearly at every page.

It was hard work for her to read at first, but the drawings enticed and helped her, and she soon sank breathlessly into the charm of the story. Many words she did not know; many passages were beyond her comprehension; she was absolutely ignorant, and had nothing but the force of her own fancy to aid her.

But though stumbling at every step, as a lame child through a flowery hillside in summer, she was happy as the child would be, because of the sweet strange air that was blowing about her, and the blossoms that she could gather into her hand, so rare, so wonderful, and yet withal so familiar, because they *were* blossoms.

With her fingers buried in her curls, with her book on her knee, with the moonrays white and strong on the page, Bébée sat entranced as the hours went by; the children's play-shouts died away, the babble of the gossip at the house doors ceased; people went by and called good-night to her; the little huts shut up one by one, like the white and purple convolvulus cups in the hedges.

Bébée did not stir, nor did she hear them; she was deaf even to the singing of the nightingales in the willows, where she sat in her little dark porch, with the ivy dropping from the thatch above, and the wet garden ways beyond her.

A heavy step came tramping down the lane. A voice called to her,—

"What are you doing, Bébée, there this time of the night? It is on the strike of twelve."

She started as if she were doing some evil thing, and stretched her arms out, and looked around with blinded wondering eyes, as if she had been rudely wakened from her sleep.

"What are you doing up so late?" asked Jeannot; he was coming from the forest in the dead of night to bring food for his family; he lost his sleep thus often, but he never thought that he did anything except his duty in those long, dark, tiring tramps to and fro between Soignies and Laeken.

Bébée shut her book and smiled with dreaming eyes, that saw him not at all.

"I was reading——and, Jeannot, his name is Flamen for the world—but I may call him Victor."

"What do I care for his name?"

"You asked it this morning."

"More fool I. Why do you read? Reading is not for poor folk like you and me."

Bébée smiled up at the white clear moon that sailed above the woods.

She was not awake out of her dream. She only dimly heard the words he spoke.

"You are a little peasant," said Jeannot roughly, as he paused at the gate. "It is all you can do to get your bread. You have no one to stand between you and hunger. How will it be with you when the slug gets your roses, and the snail your carnations, and your hens die of damp, and your lace is all wove awry, because your head runs on reading and folly, and you are spoilt for all simple pleasures, and for all honest work!"

She smiled, still looking up at the moon, with the dropping ivy touching her hair.

"You are cross, dear Jeannot. Good-night."

A moment afterwards the little rickety door was shut, and the rusty bolt drawn within it; Jeannot stood in the cool summer night all alone, and knew how stupid he had been in his wrath.

He leaned on the gate a minute; then crossed

the garden as softly as his wooden shoes would let him. He tapped gently on the shutter of the lattice.

"Bébée—Bébée—just listen. I spoke roughly, dear—I know I have no right. I am sorry. Will you be friends with me again?—do be friends again."

She opened the shutter a little way, so that he could see her pretty mouth speaking.

"Oh, Jeannot, what does it matter? Yes, we are friends—we will always be friends, of course—only you do not know. Good-night."

He went away with a heavy heart and a long-drawn step. He would have preferred that she should have been angry with him.

Bébée, left alone, let the clothes drop off her pretty round shoulders and her rosy limbs, and shook out her coils of hair, and kissed the book, and laid it under her head, and went to sleep with a smile on her face.

Only, as she slept, her fingers moved as if she were counting her beads, and her lips murmured.

"Oh, dear Holy Mother, you have so much to

think of—yes, I know—all the poor, and all the little children. But take care of *him;* he is called Flamen, and he lives in the street of Mary of Burgundy; you cannot miss him; and if you will look for him always, and have a heed that the angels never leave him, I will give you my great cactus flower—my only one—on your Feast of Roses this very year. Oh, dear Mother, you will not forget!"

## CHAPTER XL

Bébée was a dreamer in her way, and aspired to be a scholar too. But all the same, she was not a little fool.

She had been reared in hardy, simple, honest ways of living, and would have thought it as shameful as a theft to have owed her bread to other folk.

So, though she had a wakeful, restless night, full of strange phantasies, none the less was she out in her garden by daybreak; none the less did she sweep out her floor and make her mash for the fowls, and wash out her bit of linen and hang it to dry on a line amongst the tall, flaunting hollyhocks that were so proud of themselves because they reached to the roof.

"What do you want with books, Bébée?" said Reine, the sabot-maker's wife, across the privet hedge, as she also hung out her linen, "Franz told

me you were reading last night. It is the silver
buckles have done that: one mischief always begets
another."

"Where is the mischief, good Reine?" said
Bébée, who was always prettily behaved with her
elders, though, when pushed to it, she could hold
her own.

"The mischief will be in discontent," said the
sabot-maker's wife. "People live on their own little
patch, and think it is the world; that is as it should
be—everybody within his own, like a nut in its
shell. But when you get reading, you hear of a
swarm of things you never saw, and you fret because you cannot see them, and you dream, and
dream, and a hole is burnt in your soup-pot, and
your dough is as heavy as lead. You are like bees
that leave their own clover fields to buzz themselves
dead against the glass of a hothouse."

Bébée smiled, reaching to spread out her linen.
But she said nothing.

"What good is it talking to them?" she thought;
"they do not know."

Already the neighbours and friends of her infancy seemed so far, far away; creatures of a distant world, that she had long left; it was no use talking, they never would understand.

"Antoine should never have taught you your letters," said Reine, groaning under the great blue shirts she was hanging on high amongst the leaves. "I told him so at the time. I said, 'The child is a good child, and spins, and sews, and sweeps, rare and fine for her age—why go and spoil her?' But he was always headstrong. Not a child of mine knows a letter, the saints be praised; nor a word of any tongue but our own good Flemish. You should have been brought up the same. You would have come to no trouble then."

"I am in no trouble, dear Reine," said Bébée, scattering the potato peels to the clacking poultry, and she smiled into the faces of the golden oxlips that nodded to her back again in sunshiny sympathy.

"Not yet," said Reine, hanging her last shirt.

But Bébée was not hearing; she was calling the chickens, and telling the oxlips how pretty they looked in the borders; and in her heart she was counting the minutes till the old Dutch cuckoo clock at Mère Krebs—the only clock in the lane— should crow out the hour at which she went down to the city.

She loved the hut, the birds, the flowers; but they were little to her now compared with the dark golden picturesque square, the changing crowds, the frowning roofs, the grey stones, and the delight of watching through the shifting colours and shadows of the throngs for one face and for one smile.

"He is sure to be there," she thought, and started half an hour earlier than was her wont. She wanted to tell him all her rapture in the book—no one else could understand.

But all the day through he never came.

Bébée sat with a sick heart and a parched little throat, selling her flowers and straining her eyes through the tumult of the square.

The whole day went by, and there was no sign of him.

The flowers had sold well; it was a feast-day; her pouch was full of pence—what was that to her?

She went and prayed in the Cathedral, but it

seemed cold, and desolate, and empty; even the storied windows seemed dark.

"Perhaps he is gone out of the city," she thought; and a terror fell on her that frightened her; it was so unlike any fear that she had ever known—even the fear when she had seen death on old Antoine's face had been nothing like this.

Going home through the streets, she passed the café of the Trois Frères that looks out on the trees of the park, and that has flowers in its balconies, and pleasant windows that stand open to let the sounds of the soldiers' music enter. She saw him in one of the windows. There were amber and scarlet and black; silks and satins and velvets. There was a fan painted and jewelled. There were women's faces. There was a heap of purple fruit, and glittering sweetmeats. He laughed there. His beautiful Murillo head was dark against the white and gold within.

Bébée looked up—paused a second,—then went onward, with a thorn in her heart.

He had not seen her.

"It is natural, of course—he has his world—he

does not think often of me—there is no reason why he should be as good as he is," she said to herself as she went slowly over the stones.

She had the dog's soul — only she did not know it.

But the tears fell down her cheeks, as she walked.

It looked so bright in there, so gay, with the sound of the music coming in through the trees, and those women—she had seen such women before; sometimes in the winter nights, going home from the lace-work, she had stopped at the doors of the palaces, or of the opera-house, when the carriages were setting down their brilliant burdens; and sometimes on the great feast-days she had seen the people of the court going out to some gala, at the theatre, or some great review of troops, or some ceremonial of foreign sovereigns; but she had never thought about them before; she had never wondered whether velvet was better to wear than woollen serge, or diamonds lighter on the head than a little cap of linen.

But now—

Those women seemed to her so dazzlingly, so
wondrously, so superhumanly beautiful; they seemed
like some of those new dahlia flowers, rose and
purple and gold, that out-blazed the sun, on the
south border of her little garden, and blanched all
the soft colour out of the homely roses, and pim-
pernels, and sweet-williams, and double-stocks, that
had bloomed there ever since the days of Waterloo.

But, the dahlias had no scent—and Bébée wondered if these women had any heart in them—they
looked all laughter, and glitter, and vanity.  To the
child, whose dreams of womanhood were evolved
from the face of the Mary of the Assumption, of
the Susannah of Mieris, and of that Angel in the
blue coif whose face has a light as of the sun: to
her who had dreamed her way into vague percep-
tions of her own sex's maidenhood and maternity
by help of those great pictures which had been before her sight from infancy, there was some taint,
some artifice, some want, some harshness in these
jewelled women — she could not have reasoned
about it, but she felt it,—as she felt that the grand
dahlias missed a flower's divinity, being scentless.

She was a little bit of wild thyme herself; hardy, fragrant, clean, tender, flowering by the wayside, full of honey, though only nourished on the turf and the stones—these gaudy, brilliant, ruby-bright, scarlet-mantled dahlias hurt her with a dim sense of pain and shame.

Fasting, next day at sunrise she confessed to Father Francis.

"I saw beautiful rich women, and I envied them; and I could not pray to Mary last night for thinking of them—for I hated them so much."

But she did not say:

"I hated them because they were with him."

Out of the purest little soul, Love entering drives forth Candour.

"That is not like you at all, Bébée," said the good old man, as she knelt at his feet on the bricks of his little bare study, where all the books he ever spelt out, were treatises on the art of bee-keeping. "My dear, you never were covetous at all, nor did you ever seem to care for the things of the world. I wish Jehan had not given you those silver buckles; I think they have set your little soul on vanities."

"It is not the buckles; I am not covetous," said Bébée; and then her face grew warm. She did not know why, and she did not hear the rest of Father Francis's admonitions.

————

## CHAPTER XII.

BUT the next noon-time brought him to the market stall, and the next also, and so the summer days slipped away, and Bébée was quite happy if she saw him in the morning-time, to give him a fresh rose, or at evening by the gates, or under the beech-trees, when he brought her a new book, and sauntered awhile up the green lane beside her.

An innocent unconscious love like Bébée's wants so little food to make it all content. Such mere trifles are beautiful and sweet to it. Such slender stray gleams of light suffice to make a broad bright golden noon of perfect joy around it.

All the delirium, and fever, and desire, and despair, that are in maturer passion, are far away from it: far as is the flash of the meteor across sultry skies, from the blue forget-me-not down in the brown meadow brook.

It was very wonderful to Bébée that he, this

stranger from Rubes' Fairyland, could come at all
to keep pace with her little clattering wooden shoes
over the dust and the grass in the dim twilight-time.
The days went by in a trance of sweet amaze, and
she kept count of the hours no more by the cuckoo-
clock of the millhouse, or the deep chimes of the
Brussels belfries; but only by such moments as brought
her a word from his lips, or even a glimpse of him
from afar, across the crowded square.

She sat up half the nights reading the books he
gave her, studying the long cruel polysyllables, and
spelling slowly through the phrases that seemed to
her so cramped and tangled, and which yet were a
pleasure to unravel for sake of the thought they held.

For Bébée, ignorant little simple soul that she
was, had a mind in her that was eager, observant,
quick to acquire, skilful to retain; and it would
happen in certain times that Flamen, speaking to
her of the things which he gave to her to read,
would think to himself that this child had more wisdom than was often to be found in schools.

Meanwhile he pondered various studies in various
stages of a Gretchen, and made love to Bébée—

made love at least by his eyes and by his voice, not hurrying his pleasant task, but hovering about her softly, and mindful not to scare her, as a man will gently lower his hand over a poised butterfly that he seeks to kill, and which one single movement, a thought too quick, may scare away to safety.

Bébée knew where he lived in the street of Mary of Burgundy; in an old palace that belonged to a great Flemish noble, who never dwelt there himself; but to ask anything about him—why he was there? what his rank was? why he stayed in the city at all? was a sort of treason that never entered her thoughts.

Psyche, if she had been as simple and loyal as Bébée was, would never have lighted her own candle; but even Psyche would not have borrowed any one else's lamp to lighten the love darkness.

To Bébée he was sacred, unapproachable, unquestionable; he was a wonderful, perfect happiness that had fallen into her life; he was a gift of God, as the sun was.

She took his going and coming as she took that of the sun, never dreaming of reproaching his absence, never dreaming of asking if in the empty night he shone on any other worlds than hers.

It was hardly so much a faith with her as an instinct; faith must reason ere it know itself to be faith. Bébée never reasoned any more than her roses did.

The good folks in the market-place watched her a little anxiously; they thought ill of that little moss rose that every day found its way to one wearer only, but after all they did not see much, and the neighbours nothing at all. For he never went home to her, nor with her, and most of the time that he spent with Bébée was in the quiet evening shadows, as she went up with her empty basket through the deserted country roads.

Bébée was all day long in the city, indeed, as other girls were, but with her it had always been different. Antoine had always been with her up to the day of his death; and after his death she had sat in the same place, surrounded by the people she had known from infancy, and an insult to her would have been answered by a stroke from the cobbler's strap or from the tinker's hammer. There was one girl only who ever tried to do her any harm—a good-looking, stout wench, who stood at the corner of the Montagne de la Cour with a stall of fruit in the summer time, and in winter time drove a milk-cart over the snow. This girl would get at her sometimes, and talk of the students, and tell her how good it was to get out of the town on a holiday, and go to any one of the villages where there was kermesse and dance, and drink the little blue wine, and have trinkets bought for one, and come home in the moonlight in a char-à-banc, with the horns sounding, and the lads singing, and the ribbons flying from the old horse's ears.

"She is such a little close sly thing!" thought the fruit-girl, sulkily. To vice, innocence must always seem only a superior kind of chicanery.

"We dance almost every evening, the children and I," Bébée had answered when urged fifty times by this girl to go to fairs, and balls at the wine-shops. "That does just as well. And I have seen kermesse once at Malines—it was beautiful. I went with Mère Dax, but it cost a great deal I know, though she did not let me pay."

"You little fool!" the fruit-girl would say, and grin, and eat a pear.

But the good honest old women who sat about in the Grande Place, hearing, had always taken the fruit-girl to task, when they got her by herself.

"Leave the child alone, you mischievous one," said they. "Be content with being base yourself. Look you, Lisette—she is not one like you to make eyes at the law-students, and pester the painter lads for a day's outing. Let her be, or we will tell your mother how you leave the fruit for the gutter children to pick and thieve, while you are stealing up the stairs into that young French fellow's chamber. Oh, oh! a fine beating you will get when she knows."

Lisette's mother was a fierce and strong old Brabantoise, who exacted heavy reckoning with her daughter for every single plum and peach that she sent out of her dark sweet-smelling fruitshop to be sunned in the streets, and under the students' love-glances.

So the girl took heed, and left Bébée alone.

"What should I want her to come with us for?" she reasoned with herself. "She is twice as pretty as I am,—Jules might take to her instead—who knows?"

So that she was at once savage and yet triumphant when she saw, as she thought, Bébée drifting down the high flood of temptation.

"Oh, oh, you dainty one!" she cried, one day to her. "So you would not take the nuts and mulberries that do for us common folk, because you had a mind for a fine pine out of the hothouses! That was all, was it? Eh, well—I do not begrudge you. Only take care—remember, the nuts and mulberries last through summer and autumn, and there are heaps of them on every fair-stall and street-corner; but the pine—that is eaten in a day, one springtime, and its like does not grow in the hedges. You will have your mouth full of sugar an hour—and then, eh!—you will go famished all the year."

"I do not understand," said Bébée, looking up with her thoughts far away, and scarcely hearing the words spoken to her.

"Oh, pretty little fool—you understand well enough," said Lisette, grinning, as she rubbed up a melon. "Does he give you fine things?—you might let me see."

"No one gives me anything."

"Chut! you want me to believe that. Why Jules is only a lad, and his father is a silkmercer, and only gives him a hundred francs a month, but Jules buys me all I want—somehow—or do you think I would take the trouble to set my cap straight when he goes by? He gave me these ear-rings, look. I wish you would let me see what you get."

But Bébée had gone away—unheeding—dreaming of Juliet and of Jeanne d'Arc, of whom he had told her tales.

He made sketches of her sometimes, but seldom pleased himself.

It was not so easy, as he had imagined that it would prove, to pourtray this little flower-like face, with the clear eyes and the child's open brow. He who had painted Phryne so long and faithfully had got a taint on his brush—he could not paint this pure, bright, rosy dawn—he who had always painted the glare of midnight gas on rouge or rags. Yet he felt that if he could transfer to canvas the light that was on Bébée's face he would get what Scheffer had missed.  For a time it eluded him.  You shall paint a gold and glistening brocade, or a fan of peacock's feathers to perfection, and yet, perhaps, the dewy whiteness of the humble little field-daisy shall baffle and escape you.

He felt, too, that he must catch her expression flying as he would do the flash of a swallow's wing across a blue sky; he knew that Bébée, forced to studied attitudes in an atelier, would be no longer the ideal that he wanted.

More than once he came and filled in more fully his various designs in the little hut garden, amongst the sweet grey lavender and the golden disks of the sunflowers; and more than once Bébée was missed from her place in the front of the Broodhuis.

The Varnhart children would gather now and then openmouthed at the wicket, and Mère Krebs would shake her head as she went by on her sheepskin saddle, and mutter that the child's head would be turned by vanity, and old Jehan would lean on his stick and peer through the sweetbriar, and wonder stupidly if this strange man who could

make Bébée's face beam over again upon that panel
of wood could not give him back his dead daughter
who had been pushed away under the black earth
so long, long before, when the red mill had been
brave and new, the red mill that the boys and girls
called old.

But except these no one noticed much.

Painters were no rare sights in Brabant.

The people were used to see them coming and
going, making pictures of mud and stones, and
ducks and sheep, and of all common and silly
things.

"What does he pay you, Bébée?" they used to
ask, with the shrewd Flemish thought after the main
chance.

"Nothing," Bébée would answer, with a quick
colour in her face, and they would reply in con-
temptuous reproof, "Careless little fool;—you should
make enough to buy you wood all winter. When
the man from Ghent painted Trine and her cow, he
gave her a whole gold bit for standing still so long
in the clover. The Krebs would be sure to lend
you her cow if it be the cow that makes the difference."

Bébée was silent, weeding her carnation bed;—what could she tell them that they would understand?

She seemed so far away from them all—those good friends of her childhood—now that this wonderful new world of his giving had opened to her sight.

She lived in a dream.

Whether she sat in the market-place taking copper coins, or in the moonlight with a book on her knees, it was all the same. Her feet ran, her tongue spoke, her hands worked; she did not neglect her goat or her garden, she did not forsake her house labour or her good deeds to old Annémie; but all the while she only heard one voice, she only felt one touch, she only saw one face.

Here and there—one in a million—there is a female thing that can love like this, once and for ever.

Such an one is dedicated, birth upwards, to the Mater Dolorosa.

He had something nearer akin to affection for her than he had ever had in his life for anything, but he was never in love with her—no more in love with her than with the moss-rosebuds that she fastened in his breast. Yet he played with her, because she was such a little, soft, tempting, female thing; and because, to see her face flush, and her heart heave, to feel her fresh feelings stir into life, and to watch her changes from shyness to confidence, and from frankness again into fear, was a natural pastime in the lazy golden weather.

That he spared her as far as he did—when after all she would have married Jeannot anyhow,—and that he sketched her face in the open air, and never entered her hut and never beguiled her to his own old palace in the city was a new virtue in himself for which he hardly knew whether to feel respect or ridicule; anyway it seemed virtue to him.

So long as he did not seduce the body it seemed to him that it could never matter how he slew the soul—the little, honest, happy, pure, frank soul, that amidst its poverty and hardships was like a robin's song to the winter sun.

"Hoot, toot, pretty innocent, so you are no better than the rest of us," hissed her enemy, Lisette,

the fruit girl, against her as she went by the stall
one evening as the sun set. "Prut! so it was no
such purity after all that made you never look at
the student lads and the soldiers, eh?—You were so
dainty of taste, you must needs pick and choose,
and, Lord's sake, after all your coyness, to drop at a
beckoning finger as one may say—pong!—in
a minute, like an apple over-ripe! Ohhè, you sly
one!"

Bébée flushed red, in a sort of instinct of offence; not sure what her fault was, but vaguely
stung by the brutal words.

Bébée walking homeward by him, with her empty
baskets, looked at him with grave wondering eyes.

"What did she mean? I do not understand. I
must have done some wrong—or she thinks so. Do
you know?——"

Flamen laughed, and answered her evasively:

"You have done her the wrong of a fair skin
when hers is brown, and a little foot, while hers is
as big as a trooper's; there is no greater sin, Bébée,
possible in woman to woman."

"Hold your peace, you shrill jade," he added,

in anger to the fruiterer, flinging at her a crown piece, that the girl caught and bit with her teeth with a chuckle. "Do not heed her, Bébée. She is a coarse-tongued brute, and is jealous, no doubt."

"Jealous?—of what?"

The word had no meaning to Bébée.

"That I am not a student or a soldier as her lovers are."

As her lovers were! Bébée felt her face burn again. Was he her lover then? The child's innocent body and soul thrilled with a hot, sweet, delight and fear commingled.

Bébée was not quite satisfied until she had knelt down that night and asked the Master of all poor maidens to see if there were any wickedness in her heart, hidden there like a bee in a rose, and if there were to take it out and make her worthier of this wonderful new happiness in her life.

## CHAPTER XIII.

THE next day, waking with a radiant little soul as a bird in a forest wakes in summer, Bébée was all alone in the lane by the swans' water. In the grey of the dawn all the good folk except herself and lame old Jehan had tramped off to a pilgrimage, Liège way, which the bishop of the city had enjoined on all the faithful as a sacred duty.

Bébée doing her work, singing, thinking how good God was, and dreaming over a thousand fancies of the wonderful stories he had told her, and of the exquisite delight that would lie for her in watching for him all through the shining hours, Bébée felt her little heart leap like a squirrel as the voice that was the music of heaven to her called through the stillness:

"Good day, pretty one! you are as early as the lark, Bébée. I go to Mayence, so I thought I would look at you one moment as I pass."

Bébée ran down through the wet grass in a tumult of joy. She had never seen him so early in the day—never so early as this, when nobody was up and stirring except birds and beasts and peasant folk.

She did not know how pretty she looked herself; like a rain-washed wild rose; her feet gleaming with dew, her cheeks warm with health and joy; her sunny clustering hair free from the white cap and tumbling a little about her throat, because she had been stooping over the carnations.

Flamen loosed the wicket latch and thought there might be better ways of spending the day than in the grey shadows of old Mechlin.

"Will you give me a draught of water?" he asked her as he crossed the garden.

"I will give you breakfast," said Bébée, happy as a bird. She felt no shame for the smallness of her home; no confusion at the poverty of her little place; such embarrassments are born of self-consciousness, and Bébée had no more self-consciousness than her own sweet, grey lavender bush blowing against the door.

The lavender bush has no splendour like the roses, has no colours like the hollyhocks; it is a simple, plain, grey thing that the bees love and that the cottagers cherish, and that keeps the moth from the homespun linen, and that goes with the dead to their graves.

It has many virtues and infinite sweetness, but it does not know it or think of it; and if the village girls ever tell it so, it fancies they only praise it out of kindness as they put its slender fragrant spears away in their warm bosoms. Bébée was like her lavender, and now that this beautiful Purple Emperor butterfly came from the golden sunbeams to find pleasure for a second in her freshness, she was only very grateful, as the lavender bush was to the village girls.

"I will give you your breakfast," said Bébée, flushing rosily with pleasure, and putting away the ivy coils that he might enter.

"I have very little, you know," she added, wistfully. "Only goat's milk and bread; but if that will do—and there is some honey—and if you would eat a salad, I would cut one fresh."

He did enter, and glanced round him with a curious pity and wonder both in one.

It was such a little, small, square place; and its floor was of beaten clay; and its unceiled roof he could have touched; and its absolute poverty was so plain,—and yet the child looked so happy in it, and was so like a flower, and was so dainty and fresh, and even so full of grace.

She stood and looked at him with frank and grateful eyes; she could hardly believe that he was here; he, the stranger of Rubes' Land, in her own little rush-covered home.

But she was not embarrassed by it; she was glad and proud.

There is a dignity of peasants as well as of kings—the dignity that comes from all absence of effort, all freedom from pretence. Bébée had this, and she had more still than this: she had the absolute simplicity of childhood with her still.

Some women have it still when they are fourscore.

She could have looked at him for ever, she was so happy; she cared nothing now for those dazzling

dahlias—he had left them; he was actually here—
here in her own, little, dear home, with the cocks
looking in at the threshold, and the sweetpeas
nodding at the lattice, and the starling crying
"Bonjour! Bonjour!"

"You are tired, I am sure you must be tired,"
she said, pulling her little bed forward for him to
sit on, for there were only two wooden stools in
the hut, and no chair at all.

Then she took his sketching easel and brushes
from his hand, and would have kneeled and taken
the dust off his boots if he would have let her; and
went hither and thither gladly and lightly, bringing
him a wooden bowl of milk and the rest of the
slender fare, and cutting as quick as thought fresh
cresses and lettuce from her garden, and bringing
him, as the crown of all, Father Francis's honeycomb on vine-leaves, with some pretty sprays of
box and mignonette scattered about it—doing all
this with a swift, sweet grace that robbed the labour
of all look of servitude, and looking at him ever
and again with a smile that said as clearly as any

words: "I cannot do much, but what I do, I do
with all my heart."

There was something in the sight of her going
and coming in those simple household errands,
across the sunlit floor, that moved him as some
mountain air sung on an alp by a girl driving her
cows to pasture may move a listener who indifferent
has heard the swell of the organ of La Hague, or
the recitative of a great singer in San Carlo.

The grey lavender blowing at the house-door
has its charm for those who are tired of the camel-
lias that float in the porcelain bowls of midnight
suppers.

This man was not good.  He was idle and
vain, and amorous and cold, and had been spoiled
by the world in which he had passed his days; but
he had the temper of an artist; he had something,
too, of a poet's fancy; he was vaguely touched and
won by this simple soul that looked at him out of
Bébée's eyes with some look that in all its simplicity
had a divine gleam in it that made him half
ashamed.

He had known women by the thousand, good

women and bad; women whom he had dealt ill with and women who had dealt ill with him; but this he had not known—this frank, fearless, tender, gay, grave, innocent, industrious little life, helping itself, feeding itself, defending itself, working for itself and for others, and vaguely seeking all the while some unseen light, some unknown god, with a blind faith so infinitely ignorant and yet so infinitely pathetic.

"All the people are gone on a pilgrimage," she explained to him when he asked her why her village was so silent this bright morning. "They are gone to pray for a fine harvest, and then each one prays for some other little thing that she wants herself as well—it costs seven francs apiece. They take their food with them; they go and laugh and eat in the fields. I think it is nonsense. One can say one's prayers just as well here. Mère Krebs thinks so too, but then she says: 'If I do not go, it will look ill; people will say I am irreligious; and as we make so much by flour, God would think it odd for me to be absent; and, besides, it is only seven francs there and back; and if it does please

Heaven, that is cheap, you know. One will get it over and over again in Paradise.' That is what Mère Krebs says. But, for me, I think it is nonsense. It cannot please God to go by train and eat galette and waste a whole day in getting dusty.

"When I give the Virgin my cactus flower, I do give up a thing I love, and I let it wither on her altar instead of pleasing me in bloom here all the week, and then, of course, she sees that I have done it out of gratitude. But that is different: that I am sorry to do, and yet I am glad to do it out of love. Do you not know?"

"Yes, I know very well. But is the Virgin all that you love like this?"

"No; there is the garden, and there is Antoine —he is dead, I know. But I think that we should love the dead all the better, not the less, because they cannot speak or say that they are angry; and perhaps one pains them very much when one neglects them, and if they are ever so sad, they cannot rise and rebuke one—that is why I would rather forget the flowers for the Church than I would the flowers for his grave, because God can punish me, of course, if he like, but Antoine never can—any more—now."

"You are logical in your sentiment, my dear," said Flamen, who was more moved than he cared to feel. "The union is a rare one in your sex. Who taught you to reason?"

"No one. And I do not know what to be logical means. Is it that you laugh at me?"

"No. I do not laugh. And your pilgrims— they are gone for all day?"

"Yes. They are gone to the Sacred Heart at Ste. Marie en Bois. It is on the way to Liège. They will come back at nightfall. And some of them will be sure to have drunk too much, and the children will get so cross. Prosper Bar, who is a Calvinist, always says, 'Do not mix up prayer and play; you would not cut a gherkin in your honey;' but I do not know why he called prayer a gherkin, because it is sweet enough—sweeter than anything, I think. When I pray to the Virgin to let me see you next day, I go to bed quite happy, because she will do it, I know, if it will be good for me."

"But if it were not good for you, Bébée? Would.
you cease to wish it then?"

He rose as he spoke, and went across the floor
and drew away her hand that was parting the flax,
and took it in his own and stroked it, indulgently
and carelessly, as a man may stroke the soft fur of
a young cat.

Leaning against the little lattice and looking
down on her with musing eyes, half smiling, half
serious, half amorous, half sad, Bébée looked up
with a sudden and delicious terror that ran through
her as the charm of the snake's gaze runs through
the bewildered bird.

"Would you cease to wish if it were not good?"
he asked again.

Bébée's face grew pale and troubled. She left
her hand in his because she did not think any
shame of his taking it. But the question suddenly
flung the perplexity and darkness of doubt into the
clearness of her pure child's conscience. All her
ways had been straight and sunlit before her.

She had never had a divided duty.

The religion and the pleasure of her simple

little life had always gone hand-in-hand, greeting one another, and never for an instant in conflict. In any hesitation of her own she had always gone to Father Francis, and he had disentangled the web for her and made all plain.

But here was a difficulty in which she could never go to Father Francis.

Right and wrong, duty and desire, were for the first time arrayed before her in their ghastly and unending warfare.

It frightened her with a certain breathless sense of peril—the peril of a time when in lieu of that gentle Mother of Roses whom she kneeled to amongst the flowers, she would only see a dusky shadow looming between her and the beauty of life and the light of the sun.

What he said was quite vague to her. She attached no definite danger to his words. She only thought—to see him was so great a joy—if Mary forbade it, would she not take it if she could not-withstanding, always, always, always?

He kept her hand in his, and watched with

contentment the changing play of the shade and
sorrow, the fear and fascination, on her face.

"You do not know, Bébée!" he said at length,
knowing well himself; so much better than ever
she knew. "Well, dear—that is not flattering to
me. But it is natural. The good Virgin of course
gives you all you have, food, and clothes, and your
garden, and your pretty plump chickens—and I am
only a stranger. You could not offend her for me
—that is not likely."

The child was cut to the heart by the sadness
and humility of words of whose studied artifice she
had no suspicion.

She thought that she seemed to him ungrateful
and selfish, and yet all the mooring-ropes that held
her little boat of life to the harbour of its simple
religion seemed cut away, and she seemed drifting
helpless and rudderless upon an unknown sea.

"I never did do wrong—that I know," she said
timidly, and lifted her eyes to his with an unconscious appeal in them.

"But—I do not see why it should be wrong to

speak with you. You are good, and you lend me beautiful things out of other men's minds that will make me less ignorant:—Our Lady could not be angry with that—she must like it."

"Our Lady?—oh, poor little simpleton!—where will her reign be when Ignorance has once been cut down, root and branch?" he thought to himself; but he only answered—

"But whether she like it or not, Bébée?—you beg the question, my dear; you are—you are not so frank as usual—think, and tell me honestly?"

He knew quite well, but it amused him to see the perplexed trouble that this the first divided duty of her short years brought with it.

Bébée looked at him, and loosened her hand from his, and sat quite still. Her lips had a little quiver in them.

"I think," she said at last, "I think—if it *be* wrong, still I will wish it—yes. Only I will not tell myself that it is right. I will just say to Our Lady, 'I am wicked, perhaps, but I cannot help it.' So— I will not deceive her at all; and perhaps in time she may forgive. But I think you only say it to try

me. It cannot, I am sure, be wrong—any more
than it is to talk to Jeannot or to Bac."

He had driven her into the subtleties of doubt,
but the honest little soul in her found a way out, as
a flower in a cellar finds its way through the stones
to light.

He plucked the ivy leaves and threw them at
the chickens on the bricks without, with a certain
impatience in the action. The simplicity and the
directness of the answer disarmed him; he was almost ashamed to use against her the weapons of his
habitual warfare. It was like a maître d'armes
fencing with bare steel against a little naked child
armed with a blest palm-sheaf.

When she had thus brought him all she had,
and he to please her had sat down to the simple
food, she gathered a spray of roses and set it in a
pot beside him, then left him and went and stood
at a little distance, waiting, with her hands lightly
crossed on her chest, to see if there were anything
that he might want.

He ate and drank well to please her, looking at
her often as he did so.

"I break your bread, Bébée," he said, with a tone that seemed strange to her. "I break your bread. I must keep Arab faith with you."

"What is that?"

"I mean—I must never betray you."

"Betray me!  How could you?"

"Well—hurt you in any way."

"Ah, I am sure you would never do that."

He was silent, and looked at the spray of roses.

"Sit down and spin," he said impatiently. "I am ashamed to see you stand there, and a woman never looks so well as when she spins. Sit down—and I will eat the good things you have brought me. But I cannot if you stand and look."

"I beg your pardon, I did not know," she said, ashamed lest she should have seemed rude to him; and she drew out her wheel under the light of the lattice, and sat down to it, and began to disentangle the threads.

It was a pretty picture—the low, square casement; the frame of ivy, the pink and white of the climbing sweet peas; the girl's head; the cool, wet leaves; the old wooden spinning-wheel, that purred like a sleepy cat.

"I want to paint you as Gretchen, only it will be a shame," he said.

"Who is Gretchen?"

"You shall read of her by-and-by. And you live here all by yourself?"

"Since Antoine died—yes."

"And are never dull?"

"I have no time, and I do not think I would be if I had time—there is so much to think of, and one never can understand."

"But you must be very brave and laborious to do all your work yourself. Is it possible a child like you can spin, and wash, and bake, and garden, and do everything?"

"Oh, many do more than I. Babette's eldest daughter is only twelve, and she does much more, because she has all the children to look after; and they are very, very poor; they often have nothing but a stew of nettles and perhaps a few snails, days together."

"That is lean, bare, ugly, gruesome poverty;

there is plenty of that everywhere.  But you, Bébée —you are an idyll."

Bébée looked across the hut and smiled, and broke her thread.  She did not know what he meant, but if she were anything that pleased him, it was well.

"Who were those beautiful women?" she said suddenly, the colour mounting into her cheeks.

"What women, my dear?"

"Those I saw at the window with you, the other night—they had jewels."

"Oh!—women, tiresome enough; if I had seen you, I would have dropped you some fruit.  Poor little Bébée!  Did you go by, and I never knew?"

"You were laughing——"

"Was I?"

"Yes, and they *were* beautiful."

"In their own eyes; not in mine."

"No?"

She stopped her spinning and gazed at him with wistful, wondering eyes.  Could it be that they were not beautiful to him? those deep-red, glowing, sun-basked dahlia flowers?

"Do you know," she said very softly, with a
flush of penitence that came and went, "when I
saw them, I hated them; I confessed it to Father
Francis next day. You seemed so content with
them, and they looked so gay and glad there—and
then the jewels! Somehow, I seemed to myself such
a little thing, and so ugly and mean. And yet, do
you know——"

"And yet—well?"

"They did not look to me good—those women," said Bébée, thoughtfully, looking across at
him in deprecation of his possible anger. "They
were great people, I suppose, and they appeared
very happy; but though I seemed nothing to myself
after them, still I think I would not change."

"You are wise without books, Bébée."

"Oh, no—I am not wise at all. I only feel.
And give me books; oh, pray, give me books! You
do not know; I will learn so fast—and I will not
neglect anything,—that I promise. The neighbours
and Jeannot say that I shall let the flowers die, and
the hut get dirty, and never spin or prick Annémie's
patterns; but that is untrue. I will do all, just as I

have done, and more too, if only you will give me
things to read, for I do think, when one is happy,
one ought to work more—not less."

"But will these books make you happy? If you
ask me the truth, I must tell you—no. You are
happy as you are, because you know nothing else
than your own little life; for ignorance *is* happiness,
Bébée, let sages, ancient and modern, say what they
will. But when you know a little, you will want to
know more; and when you know much, you will
want to see much also, and then—and then—the
thing will grow—you will be no longer content.
That is, you will be unhappy."

Bébée watched him with wistful eyes.

"Perhaps that is true. No doubt it is true, if you
say it. But you know all the world seems full of
voices that I hear, but that I cannot understand; it
is with me as I should think it is with people who
go to foreign countries and do not know the tongue
that is spoken when they land; and it makes me
unhappy, because I cannot comprehend, and so the
books will not make me more so, but less. And as
for being content—when I thought you were gone

away out of the city, last night, I thought I would never be able to pray any more, because I hated myself, and I almost hated the angels, and I told Mary that she was cruel, and she turned her face from me—as it seemed, for ever."

She spoke quite quietly and simply, spinning as she spoke, and looking across at him with earnest eyes, that begged him to believe her. She was saying the pure truth, but she did not know the force or the meaning of that truth.

He listened with a smile; it was not new to him; he knew her heart much better than she knew it herself, but there was an unconsciousness, and yet a strength, in the words that touched him though.

He threw the leaves away, irritably, and told her to leave off her spinning.

"Some day I shall paint you with that wheel as I painted the Broodhuis. Will you let me, Bébée?"

"Yes."

She answered him as she would have answered,

if he had told her to go on pilgrimage from one
end of the Low Countries to the other.

"What were you going to do to-day?"

"I am going into the market with the flowers; I
go every day."

"How much will you make?"

"Two or three francs, if I am lucky."

"And do you never have a holiday?"

"Oh, yes; but not often, you know, because it is on
the fête-days that the people want the most flowers."

"But in the winter?"

"Then I work at the lace."

"Do you never go into the woods?"

"I have been, once or twice; but it loses a
whole day."

"You are afraid of not earning?"

"Yes. Because I am afraid of owing people
anything."

"Well, give up this one day, and we will make
holiday. The people are out; they will not know.
Come into the forest, and we will dine at a café
in the woods; and we will be as poetic as you like,
and I will tell you a tale of one called Rosalind,

who pranked herself in boy's attire, all for love, in
the Ardennes country yonder. Come, it is the
very day for the forest; it will make me a lad again
at Meudon, when the lilacs were in bloom. Poor
Paris! Come."

"Do you mean it?"

The colour was bright in her face, her heart
was dancing, her little feet felt themselves already
on the fresh green turf.

She had no thought that there could be any
harm in it. She would have gone with Jeannot or
old Bac.

"Of course I mean it. Come. I was going to
Mayence to see the Magi and Van Dyck's Christ.
We will go to Soignies instead, and study green
leaves. I will paint your face by sunlight. It is
the best way to paint you. You belong to the
open air. So should Gretchen; or how else should
she have the blue sky in her eyes?"

"But I have only wooden shoes!"

Her face was scarlet as she glanced at her feet;
he who had wanted to give her the silk stockings
—how would he like to be seen walking abroad

with those two clumsy, clattering, work-a-day, little sabots?

"Never mind. My dear, in my time I have had enough of satin shoes and of silver-gilt heels; they click-clack as loud as yours, and cost much more to those who walk with them, not to mention that they will seldom deign to walk at all. Your wooden shoes are picturesque. Paganini made a violin out of a wooden shoe. Who knows what music may lurk in yours, only you have never heard it? Perhaps I have. It was Bac who gave you the red shoes that was the barbarian, not I. Come."

"You really mean it?"

"Come."

"But they will miss me at market?"

"They will think you are gone on the pilgrimage: you need never tell them you have not."

"But if they ask me?"

"Does it never happen that you say any other thing than the truth?"

"Any other thing than the truth! Of course not. People take for granted that one tells truth; it would be very base to cheat them. Do you

really mean that I may come?—in the forest!—and
you will tell me stories like those you give me to
read?"

"I will tell you a better story. Lock your hut,
Bébée, and come."

"And to think you are not ashamed!"

"Ashamed?"

"Yes, because of my wooden shoes."

Was it possible? Bébée thought, as she ran
out into the garden and locked the door behind
her, and pushed the key under the water-butt as
usual, being quite content with that prudent pre-
caution against robbers which had served Antoine
all his days.  Was it possible, this wonderful joy?
—her cheeks were like her roses, her eyes had a
brilliance like the sun; the natural grace and mirth
of the child blossomed in a thousand ways and
gestures.

As she went by the shrine in the wall, she bent
her knee a moment and made the sign of the
cross; then she gathered a little moss-rose that
nodded close under the border of the palisade, and
turned and gave it to him.

"Look, she sends you this.  She is not angry, you see, and it is much more pleasure when she is pleased—do you not know?"

He shrank a little as her fingers touched him.

"What a pity you had no mother, Bébée!" he said, on an impulse of emotion, of which in Paris he would have been more ashamed than of any guilt.

## CHAPTER XIV.

IN the deserted lane by the swans' water, under the willows, the horses waited to take him to Mechlin; little, quick, rough horses, with round brass bells, in the Flemish fashion, and gay harness, and a low char-à-banc, in which a wolfskin and red rugs, and all a painter's many necessities were tossed together.

He lifted her in, and the little horses flew fast through the green country, ringing chimes at each step, till they plunged into the deep glades of the woods of Cambre and Soignies.

Bébée sat breathless with delight.

She had never gone behind horses in all her life, except once or twice in a waggon when the tired teamsters had dragged a load of corn across the plains, or when the miller's old grey mare had hobbled wearily before a cartload of noisy, happy, mischievous children going home from the masses and fairs, and flags and flowers, and church banners, and puppet-shows, and lighted altars, and whirling merry-go-rounds of the Fête Dieu.

She had never known what it was to sail as on the wings of the wind along broad roads, with yellow wheat-lands, and green hedges, and wayside trees, and little villages, and reedy canal-water, all flying by her to the singsong of the joyous bells.

"Oh, how good it is to live!" she cried, clapping her hands in a very ecstacy, as the clear morning broadened into gold and the west wind rose and blew from the sands by the sea.

"Yes—it is good—if one did not tire so soon," said he, watching her with a listless pleasure.

But she did not hear; she was beyond the reach of any power to sadden her; she was watching the white oxen that stood on the purple brow of the just reapen lands, and the rosy clouds that blew like a shower of apple-blossoms across the sky to the south.

There was a sad darkling Calvary on the edge of the harvest field that looked black against the blue sky; its shadow fell across the road, but she did not see it: she was looking at the sun.

There is not much change in the great Soignies
woods. They are aisles on aisles of beautiful green
trees, crossing and recrossing; tunnels of dark
foliage that look endless; long avenues of beech, of
oak, of elm, or of fir, with the bracken and the
brushwood growing dense between; a delicious
forest growth everywhere, shady even at noon, and,
by a little past midday, dusky as evening; with the
forest fragrance, sweet and dewy, all about, and
under the fern the stirring of wild game, and the
white gleam of little rabbits, and the sound of the
wings of birds.

Soignies is not legend-haunted like the Black
Forest, nor king-haunted like Fontainebleau, nor
sovereign of two historic streams like the brave
woods of Heidelberg; nor wild and romantic, and
broken with black rocks, and poetised by the shade
of Jaques, and swept through by a perfect river,
like its neighbours of Ardennes; nor throned aloft
on mighty mountains like the majestic oak glades
of the Swabian hills of the ivory-carvers.

Soignies is only a Flemish forest in a plain,
throwing its shadow over corn-fields and cattle-

pastures, with no panorama beyond it and no wonders in its depth. But it is a fresh, bold, beautiful forest for all that.

It has only green leaves to give—green leaves always, league after league; but there is about it that vague mystery which all forests have, and this universe of leaves seems boundless, and Pan might dwell in it, and St. Hubert, and John Keats.

Bébée, in her rare holidays with the Bac children or with Jeannot's sisters, had never penetrated farther than the glades of the Cambre, and had never entered the heart of the true forest, which is much still what it must have been in the old days when the burghers of Brabant cut their yew bows and their pike-staves from it to use against the hosts of Spain.

To Bébée it was as an enchanted land, and every play of light and shade, every hare speeding across the paths, every thrush singing in the leaves, every little dog-rose or harebell that blossomed in the thickets, was to her a treasure, a picture, a poem, a delight.

He had seen girls thus in the woods of Vin-

cennes and of Versailles in the student days of his
youth; little work-girls fresh from châlets of the
Jura or from vine-hung huts of the Loire, who had
brought their poor little charms to perish in Paris;
and who dwelt under the hot tiles and amidst the
gilded shop-signs till they were as pale and thin as
their own starved balsams; and who, when they
saw the green woods, laughed and cried a little,
and thought of the broad sun-swept fields, and
wished that they were back again behind their drove
of cows, or weeding amongst the green grapes.

But those little work-girls had been mere homely
daisies, and daisies already with the dust of the
pavement and of the dancing-gardens upon them.

Bébée was as pure and fresh as these dew-
wet dog-roses that she found in the thickets of
thorn.

He had meant to treat her as he had used to
do those work-girls—a little wine, a little wooing,
a little folly and passion, idle as a butterfly and
brief as a rainbow—one midsummer day and night
—then a handful of gold, a caress, a good-morrow,
and forgetfulness ever afterwards—that was what he

had meant when he had brought her out to the forest of Soignies.

But—she was different, this child

He made the great sketch of her for his Gretchen, sitting on a moss-ground trunk, with marguerites in her hand; he sent for their breakfast far into the woods, and saw her set her pearly teeth into early peaches and costly sweetmeats; he wandered with her hither and thither, and told her tales out of the poets, and talked to her in the dreamy, cynical, poetical manner that was characteristic of him, being half artificial and half sorrowful, as his temper was.

But Bébée—all unconscious, intoxicated with happiness, and yet touched by it into that vague sadness which the summer sun brings with it even to young things, if they have soul in them;—Bébée said to him what the work-girls of Paris never had done.

Beautiful things: things fantastic, ignorant, absurd, very simple, very unreasonable oftentimes, but things beautiful always, and sometimes even very wise by a wisdom not of the world; by a certain light divine that does shine now and then as through an alabaster lamp, through minds that have no grossness to obscure them.

Her words were not equal to the burden of her thoughts at times, but he knew how to take the pearl of the thought from the broken shell and tangled seaweed of her simple, untutored speech.

"If there be a God anywhere," he thought to himself, "this little Fleming is very near him."

She was so near that, although he had no belief in any God, he could not deal with her as he had used to do with the work-girls in the primrose paths of old Vincennes.

## CHAPTER XV.

"To be Gretchen, you must count the leaves of your daisies," he said to her, as he painted—painted her just as she was, with her two little white feet in the wooden shoes, and the thick, green leaves behind; the simplest picture possible, the dress of grey—only cool dark grey—with white linen bodice, and no colour anywhere except in the green of the foliage; but where he meant the wonder and the charm of it to lie was in the upraised, serious, childlike face, and the gaze of the grave, smiling eyes.

It was Gretchen, spinning, out in the open air amongst the flowers. Gretchen, with the tall dog daisies growing up about her feet, amongst the thyme and the roses, before she had had need to gather one to ask her future of its parted leaves.

The Gretchen of Scheffer tells no tale; she is a fair-haired, hard-working, simple-minded peasant, with whom neither angels nor devils have anything to do, and whose eyes never can open to either hell or heaven. But the Gretchen of Flamen said much more than this: looking at it, men would sigh from shame, and women weep from sorrow.

"Count the daisies?" echoed Bébée. "Oh, I know what you mean. A little—much—passionately—until death—not at all. What the girls say when they want to see if anyone loves them? Is that it?"

She looked at him without any consciousness—except as she loved the flowers.

"Do you think the daisies know?" she went on, seriously, parting their petals with her fingers. "Flowers do know many things—that is certain."

"Ask them for yourself."

"Ask them what?"

"How much—anyone—loves you."

"Oh, but everyone loves me; there is no one that is bad. Antoine used to say to me, 'Never think of yourself, Bébée; always think of other people, so everyone will love you.' And I always try to do that, and everyone does."

"But that is not the love the daisy tells of to your sex."

"No?"

"No; the girls that you see count the flowers— they are thinking, not of all the village, but of some one unlike all the rest, whose shadow falls across theirs in the moonlight! You know that?"

"Ah, yes—and they marry afterwards—yes."

She said it softly, musingly, with no embarrassment; it was an unreal, remote thing to her, and yet it stirred her heart a little with a vague trouble that was infinitely sweet.

There is little talk of love in the lives of the poor; they have no space for it; love to them means more mouths to feed, more wooden shoes to buy, more hands to dive into the meagre bag of coppers. Now and then a girl of the commune had been married, and had gone out just the same the next day to her ploughing in the fields or to her lace-weaving in the city. Bébée had thought little of it.

"They marry or they do not marry. That is as it may be," said Flamen, with a smile. "Bébée, I must paint you as Gretchen before she made a love-dial of the daisies. What is the story? Oh, I have told you stories enough. Gretchen's you would not understand, just yet."

"But what did the daisies say to her?"

"My dear, the daisies always say the same thing, because daisies always tell the truth and know men. The daisies always say 'a little'; it is the girl's ear that tricks her, and makes her hear 'till death,'—a folly and falsehood of which the daisy is not guilty."

"But who says it if the daisy do not?"

"Ah, the devil perhaps—who knows? He has so much to do in these things."

But Bébée did not smile; she had a look of horror in her blue eyes; she belonged to a peasantry who believed in exorcising the fiend by the aid of the cross, and who not so very many generations before had driven him out of human bodies by rack and flame.

She looked with a little wistful fear on the white, golden-eyed marguerites that lay on her lap.

"Do you think the fiend is in these?" she whispered, with awe in her voice.

Flamen smiled. "When you count them he will be there, no doubt."

Bébée threw them with a shudder on the grass.

"Have I spoilt your holiday, dear?" he said, with a certain self-reproach.

She was silent a minute, then she gathered up the daisies again, and stroked them and put them to her lips.

"It is not they that do wrong. You say the girls' ears deceive them. It is the girls, who want a lie and will not believe a truth because it humbles them, it is the girls that are to blame; not the daisies. As for me, I will not ask the daisies anything ever, so the fiend will not enter into them."

"Nor into you. Poor little Bébée!"

"Why, you pity me for that?"

"Yes. Because, if women never see the serpent's face, neither do they ever scent the smell of the paradise roses; and it will be hard for you to die without a single rose d'amour in your pretty breast, poor little Bébée!"

"I do not understand. But you frighten me a little."

He rose and left his easel and threw himself at her feet on the grass; he took the little wooden shoes in his hands as reverently as he would have taken the broidered shoes of a duchess; he looked up at her with tender, smiling eyes.

"Poor little Bébée!" he said again. "Did I frighten you indeed! Nay, that was very base of me. We will not spoil our summer holiday. There is no such thing as a fiend, my dear. There are only men—such as I am. Say the daisy spell over for me, Bébée. See if I do not love you a little, just as you love your flowers."

She smiled, and the happy laughter came again over her face.

"Oh, I am sure you care for me a little," she said, softly, "or you would not be so good and get me books and give me pleasure; and I do not want the daisies to tell me that, because you say it yourself, which is better."

"Much better," he answered her, dreamily, and

lay there in the grass, holding the little wooden shoes in his hands.

He was not in love with her. He was in no haste. He preferred to play with her softly, slowly, as one separates the leaves of a rose, to see the deep rose of its heart.

Her own ignorance of what she felt had a charm for him. He liked to lift the veil from her eyes by gentle degrees, watching each new pulse beat, each fresh instinct tremble into life.

It was an old, old story to him; he knew each chapter and verse to weariness, though there was no other story that he still read as often. But to her it was so new.

To him it was a long beaten track; he knew every turn of it; he recognised every wayside blossom; he had passed over a thousand times each tremulous bridge; he knew so well beforehand where each shadow would fall, and where each fresh bud would blossom, and where each harvest would be reaped.

But to her it was so new.

She followed him as a blind child a man that

14*

guides her through a garden and reads her a wonder-tale.

He was good to her, that was all she knew. When he touched her ever so lightly she felt a happiness so perfect, and yet so unintelligible, that she could have wished to die in it.

And in her humility and her ignorance she wondered always how he — so great, so wise, so beautiful — could have thought it ever worth his while to leave the paradise of Rubes' Land to wait with her under her little rush-thatched roof, and bring her here to see the green leaves and the living things of the forest.

As they went, a man was going under the trees with a load of wood upon his back. Bébée gave a little cry of recognition.

"Oh, look, that is Jeannot! How he will wonder to see me here!"

Flamen drew her a little downward, so that the forester passed onward without perceiving them.

"Why do you do that?" said Bébée. "Shall I not speak to him?"

"Why? To have all your neighbours chatter of your feast in the forest? It is not worth while."

"Ah, but I always tell them everything," said Bébée, whose imagination had been already busy with the wonders that she would unfold to Mère Krebs and the Varnhart children.

"Then you will see but little of me, my dear. Learn to be silent, Bébée. It is a woman's first duty, though her hardest."

"Is it?"

She did not speak for some time. She could not imagine a state of things in which she would not narrate the little daily miracles of her life to the good old garrulous women and the little open-mouthed romps. And yet — she lifted her eyes to his.

"I am glad you have told me that," she said. "Though, indeed, I do not see why one should not say what one does, yet—somehow—I do not like to talk about you. It is like the pictures in the galleries, and the music in the Cathedral, and the great still evenings, when the fields are all silent,

and it is as if Christ walked abroad in them;—I
do not know how to talk of those things to the
others—only to you—and I do not like to talk
*about* you to them—do you not know?"

"Yes, I know. But what affinity have I, Bébée,
to your thoughts of your God walking in His corn-
fields?"

Bébée's eyes glanced down through the green
aisle of the forests, with the musing seriousness in
them that was like the child-angels of Botticelli's
dreams.

"I cannot tell you very well. But when I am
in the fields at evening and think of Christ, I feel
so happy, and of such good-will to all the rest, and
I seem to see heaven quite plain through the
beautiful grey air where the stars are—and so I feel
when I am with you—that is all. Only——"

"Only what?"

"Only in those evenings, when I was all alone,
heaven seemed up there, where the stars are, and I
longed for wings; but now, it is *here*—and I
would only shut my wings if I had them, and not
stir."

He looked at her, and took her hands and kissed them—but reverently—as a believer may kiss a shrine. In that moment to Flamen she was sacred; in that moment he could no more have hurt her with passion than he could have hurt her with a blow.

It was an emotion with him, and did not endure. But, whilst it lasted, it was true.

## CHAPTER XVI.

THEN he took her to dine at one of the wooden cafés under the trees. There was a little sheet of water in front of it, and a gay garden around. There was a balcony and a wooden stairway; there were long trellised arbours, and little white tables, and great rosebushes, like her own at home. They had an arbour all to themselves; a cool sweet-smelling bower of green, with a glimpse of scarlet from the flowers of some twisting beans.

They had a meal, the like of which she had never seen; such a huge melon in the centre of it, and curious wines, and coffee or cream in silver pots, or what looked like silver to her — "just like the altar-vases in the church," she said to herself.

"If only the Varnhart children were here!" she cried; but he did not echo the wish.

It was just sunset. There was a golden glow

on the little bit of water.  On the other side of the garden, some one was playing a guitar.  Under a lime-tree some girls were swinging, crying Higher higher! at each toss.

In a longer avenue of trellised green, at a long table, there was a noisy party of students and girls of the city; their laughter was mellowed by distance as it came over the breadth of the garden, and they sang, with fresh shrill Flemish voices, songs from an opera-bouffe of La Monnaie.

It was all pretty, and gay, and pleasant.

There was everywhere about an air of light-hearted enjoyment.  Bébée sat with a wondering look in her wide-opened eyes, and all the natural instincts of her youth, that were like curled-up fruit-buds in her, unclosed softly to the light of joy.

"Is life always like this in your Rubes' Land?" she asked him; that vague far-away country of which she never asked him anything more definite, and which yet was so clear before her fancy.

"Yes," he made answer to her.  "Only—instead

of those leaves, flowers and pomegranates; and in lieu of that tinkling guitar, a voice whose notes are esteemed like kings' jewels; and in place of those little green arbours, great white palaces, cool and still, with ilex woods and orange groves, and sapphire seas beyond them. Would you like to come there, Bébée?—and wear laces such as you weave, and hear singing and laughter all night long, and never work any more in the mould of the garden, or spin any more at that tiresome wheel, or go any more out in the wind, and the rain and the winter mud to the market?"

Bébée listened, leaning her round elbows on the table, and her warm cheeks on her hands, as a child gravely listens to a fairy story. But the sumptuous picture, and the sensuous phrase he had chosen, passed by her.

It is of no use to tempt the little chaffinch of the woods with a ruby instead of a cherry. The bird is made to feed on the brown berries, on the morning dews, on the scarlet hips of roses, and the blossoms of the wind-tossed pear-boughs; the gem, though it be a monarch's, will only strike hard and tasteless on its beak.

"I would like to see it all," said Bébée, musingly trying to follow out her thoughts. "But as for the garden work and the spinning—that I do not want to leave, because I have done it all my life; and I do not think I should care to wear lace—it would tear very soon; one would be afraid to run; and do you see I know how it is made—all that lace. I know how blind the eyes get over it, and how the hearts ache; I know how the old women starve, and the little children cry; I know that there is not a sprig of it that is not stitched with pain; the great ladies do not think, I dare say, because they have never worked at it or watched the others; but I have. And so, you see, I think if I wore it I should feel sad, and if a nail caught on it I should feel as if it were tearing the flesh of my friends. Perhaps I say it badly—but that is what I feel."

"You do not say it badly—you speak well, for you speak from the heart," he answered her, and felt a tinge of shame that he had tempted her with

the gold and purple of a baser world than any that
she knew.

"And yet you want to see new lands?" he
pursued. "What is it you want to see there?"

"Ah, quite other things than these," cried Bébée,
still leaning her cheeks on her hands. "That dancing and singing is very pretty and merry, but it is
just as good when old Claude fiddles, and the children skip. This wine you tell me is something
very great—but fresh milk is much nicer, I think.
It is not these kind of things I want—I want to
know all about the people who lived before us; I
want to know what the stars are, and what the wind
is; I want to know where the lark goes when you
lose him out of sight against the sun; I want to
know how the old artists got to see God, that they
could paint Him and all his angels as they have
done; I want to know how the voices got into the
bells, and how they can make one's heart beat,
hanging up there as they do, all alone amongst the
jackdaws; I want to know what it is when I walk
in the fields in the morning, and it is all grey, and
soft, and still, and the corn-crake cries in the wheat,

and the little mice run home to their holes, that
makes me so glad and yet so sorrowful, as if I
were so very near God, and yet so all alone, and
such a little thing; because you see the mouse she
has her hole, and the crake her own people, but
I ——"                                                    .

Her voice faltered a little and stopped, she had
never before thought out into words her own lone-
liness; from the long green arbour the voices of the
girls and the students sang—

"Ah! le doux son d'un baiser tendre!"

Flamen was silent.  The poet in him—and in
an artist there is always more or less of the poet—
kept him back from ridicule, nay, moved him to
pity and respect.

They were absurdly simple words no doubt, had
little wisdom in them, and were quite childish in
their utterance, and yet they moved him curiously
as a man very base and callous may at times be
moved by the look in a dying deer's eyes, or by
the sound of a song that some lost love once
sang.

He rose and drew her hands away, and took
her small face between his own hands instead.

"Poor little Bébée!" he said gently, looking down
on her with a breath that was almost a sigh.
"Poor little Bébée!—to envy the corn-crake and the
mouse!"

She was a little startled; her cheeks grew very
warm under his touch, but her eyes looked still into
his without fear.

He stooped and touched her forehead with his
lips, gently and without passion, almost reverently;
she grew rose-hued as the bright beanflowers, up to
the light gold ripples of her hair; she trembled a
little and drew back, but she was not alarmed
nor yet ashamed; she was too simple of heart to
feel the fear that is born of passion and of consciousness.

It was as Jeannot kissed his sister Marie, who
was fifteen years old and sold milk for the Krebs
people in the villages with a little green cart and a
yellow dog—no more.

And yet the sunny arbour leaves and the glimpse
of the blue sky swam round her indistinctly, and

the sounds of the guitar grew dull upon her ear and were lost as in a rushing hiss of water, because of the great sudden unintelligible happiness that seemed to bear her little life away on it as a sea wave bears a young child off its feet.

"You do not feel alone now, Bébée?" he whispered to her.

"No!" she answered him softly under her breath, and sat still, while all her body quivered like a leaf.

No! how could she ever be alone now that this sweet, soft, unutterable touch would always be in memory upon her; how could she wish ever again now to be the corn-crake in the summer corn or the grey mouse in the hedge of hawthorn?

At that moment a student went by past the entrance of the arbour; he had a sash round his loins and a paper feather in his cap; he was playing a fife and dancing; he glanced in as he went.

"It is time to go home, Bébée," said Flamen.

## CHAPTER XVII.

So it came to pass that Bébée's day in the big forest came and went as simply almost as any day that she had played away with the Varnhart children under the beech shadows of Cambre woods.

And when he took her to her hut at sunset before the pilgrims had returned there was a great bewildered tumult of happiness in her heart, but there was no memory with her that prevented her from looking at the shrine in the wall as she passed it, and saying with a quick gesture of the cross on brow and bosom:

"Ah, dear Holy Mother—how good you have been! and I am back again, you see, and I will work harder than ever because of all this joy that you have given me."

And she took another moss rose and changed it for that of the morning, which was faded, and said to Flamen:

"Look—she sends you this. Now do you know what I mean? One is more content when She is content."

He did not answer, but he held her hands against him a moment as they fastened in the rosebud.

"Not a word to the pilgrims, Bébée—you remember?"

"Yes, I will remember. I do not tell them every time I pray—it will be like being silent about that —it will be no more wrong than that."

But there was a touch of anxiety in the words; she was not quite certain; she wanted to be reassured. Instinct moved her not to speak of him: but habit made it seem wrong to her to have any secret from the people who had been about her from her birth.

He did not reassure her; her anxiety was pretty to watch, and he left the trouble in her heart like a bee in the chalice of a lily. Besides, the little wicket-gate was between them; he was musing whether he would push it open once more.

Her fate was in the balance, though she did not dream it: he had dealt with her tenderly, honestly, sacredly all that day—almost as much so as stupid

Jeannot could have done. He had been touched by her trust in him, and by the unconscious beauty of her fancies, into a mood that was unlike all his life and habits. But after all, he said to himself—

After all!—

Where he stood in the golden evening he saw the rosy curled mouth, the soft troubled eyes, the little brown hands that still tried to fasten the rose-bud, the young peach-like skin where the wind stirred the bodice;—she was only a little Flemish peasant, this poor little Bébée, a little thing of the fields and the streets, for all the dreams of God that abode with her. After all—soon or late—the end would be always the same. What matter!

She would weep a little to-morrow, and she would not kneel any more at the shrine in the garden wall; and then—and then—she would stay here and marry the good boor Jeannot, just the same after a while; or drift away after him to Paris, and leave her two little wooden shoes, and her visions of Christ in the fields at evening, behind her for evermore, and do as all the others did, and take not only silken stockings but the Cinderella slipper that is called Gold, which brings all other good things in its train;—what matter!

He had meant this from the first, because she was so pretty, and those little wooden sabots ran so lithely over the stones; though he was not in love with her, but only idly stretched his hand for her as a child by instinct stretches to a fruit that hangs in the sun a little rosier and a little nearer than the rest.

What matter—he said to himself—she loved him, poor little soul, though he did not know it— and there would always be Jeannot glad enough of a handful of bright French gold.

He pushed the gate gently against her; her hands fastened the rosebud and drew open the latch themselves.

"Will you come in a little?" she said, with the happy light in her face. "You must not stay long, because the flowers must be watered, and then there are Annémie's patterns—they must be done or she will have no money and so no food—but if you would come in for a little? And see—if you wait a minute I will show you the roses that I shall cut

15*

to-morrow the first thing, and take down to S. Guido to Our Lady's altar in thank-offering for to-day. I should like you to choose them—you yourself—and if you would just touch them I should feel as if you gave them to her too. Will you?"

She spoke with the pretty out-spoken frankness of her habitual speech, just tempered and broken with the happy, timid hesitation, the curious sense at once of closer nearness and of greater distance, that had come on her since he had kissed her amongst the bright bean-flowers.

He turned from her quickly.

"No, dear—no. Gather your roses alone, Bébée —if I touch them their leaves will fall."

Then with a hurriedly backward glance down the dusky lane to see that none were looking he bent his head and kissed her again quickly, and with a sort of shame, and swung the gate behind him and went away through the boughs and the shadows.

## CHAPTER XVIII.

BÉBÉE looked after him wistfully till his figure was lost in the gloom.

The village was very quiet; a dog barking afar off, and a cow lowing in the meadow, were the only living things that made their presence heard; the pilgrims had not returned.

She leaned on the gate a few minutes in that indistinct, dreamy happiness which is the prerogative of innocent love.

"How wonderful it is that he should give a thought to me!" she said again and again to herself. It was as if a king had stooped for a little knot of daisied grass to set it in his crown where the great diamonds should be.

She did not reason. She did not question. She did not look beyond that hour—such is the privilege of youth.

"How I will read! How I will learn! How wise I will try to be; and how good, if I can!" she thought, swaying the little gate lightly under her weight, and looking with glad eyes at the goats as they frisked with their young in the pasture on the other side of the big trees, whilst one by one the stars came out, and an owl hooted from the palace woods, and the frogs croaked good-nights in the rushes.

Then, like a little day-labourer as she was, with the habit of toil and the need of the poor upon her from her birth up, she shut down the latch of the gate, kissed it where his hand had rested, and went to the well to draw its nightly draught for the dry garden.

"Oh, dear roses!" she said to them as she rained the silvery showers over their nodding heads. "Oh, dear roses!—tell me—was ever anybody so happy as I am? Oh, if you say 'yes' I shall tell you you lie; silly flowers that were only born yesterday!"

But the roses shook the water off them in the wind, and said, as she wished them to say,—

"No—no one—ever before, Bébée—no one ever before."

For roses, like everything else upon earth, only speak what our own heart puts into them.

An old man went past up the lane; old Jehan,
who was too ailing and aged to make one of the
pilgrimage.  He looked at the little quick-moving
form, greyish white in the starlight, with the dark
copper vessel balanced on her head, going to and
fro betwixt the well and the garden.

"You did not go to the pilgrimage, poor little
one!" he said across the sweetbriar hedge.  "Nay,
that was too bad; work, work, work—thy pretty
back should not be bent double yet.  You want a
holiday, Bébée; well, the Fête Dieu is near.  Jeannot
shall take you, and maybe I can find a few sous for
gingerbread and merry-go-rounds.  You sit dull in
the market all day; you want a feast."

Bébée coloured behind the hedge, and ran in
and brought three new-laid eggs that she had left
in the flour-bin in the early morning, and thrust
them on him through a break in the briar.  It was
the first time she had ever done anything of which
she might not speak; she was ashamed, and yet the
secret was so sweet to her.

"I am very happy, Jehan, thank God!" she murmured, with a tremulous breath and a shine in her

eyes that the old man's ears and sight were too dull to discern.

"So was *she*," muttered Jehan, as he thrust the eggs into his old patched blue blouse. "So was she. And then a stumble—a blow in the lane there—a horse's kick—and all was over. All over, my pretty one—for ever and ever."

## CHAPTER XIX.

On a sudden impulse Flamen, going through the woodland shadows to the City, paused and turned back; all his impulses were quick, and swayed him now hither now thither in many contrary ways.

He knew that the hour was come—that he must leave her and spare her, as to himself he phrased it, or teach her the love-words that the daisies whisper to women!

And why not?—any way she would marry Jeannot.

He, half-way to the town, walked back again and paused a moment at the gate; an emotion half pitiful, half cynical, stirred in him.

Any way he would leave her in a few days; Paris had again opened her arms to him; his old life awaited him; women, who claimed him by imperious amorous demands, reproached him; and after all this day he had got the Gretchen of his ideal, a great picture for the future of his fame.

As he would leave her any way so soon, he would leave her unscathed—poor little field flower —he could never take it with him to blossom or wither in Paris.

His world would laugh too utterly if he made for himself a mistress out of a little Fleming in two wooden shoes. Besides——

Besides, something that was half weak and half noble moved him not to lead this child, in her trust and her ignorance, into ways that when she awakened from her trance would seem to her shameful and full of sorrow. For he knew that Bébée was not as others are.

He turned back and knocked at the hut door and opened it.

Bébée was just beginning to undress herself; she had taken off her white kerchief and her wooden shoes; her pretty shoulders and her little neck shone white in the moon; her feet were bare on the mud floor.

She started with a cry, and threw the handkerchief again on her shoulders, but there was no fear of him; only the unconscious instinct of her girlhood.

He thought for a moment that he would not go away until the morrow——.

"Did you want me?" said Bébée softly, with happy eyes of surprise and yet a little startled, fearing some evil might have happened to him that he should have returned thus.

"No; I do not want you, dear," he said gently; no—he did not want her, poor little soul; she wanted him, but he—there were so many of these things in his life and he liked her too well to love her.

"No, dear, I did not want you," said Flamen, drawing her arms about him, and feeling her flutter like a little bird, while the moonlight came in through the green leaves and fell in fanciful patterns on the floor. "But I came to say—you have had one happy day, wholly happy, have you not, poor little Bébée?"

"Ah, yes!" she sighed rather than said the answer in her wondrous gladness; drawn there close to him, with the softness of his lips upon her. Could he have come back only to ask that?

"Well, that is something. You will remember it always, Bébée?" he murmured in his unconscious cruelty. "I did not wish to spoil your cloudless pleasure, dear—for you care for me a little, do you not?—so I came back to tell you only now that I go away for a little while to-morrow."

"Go away!"

She trembled in his arms and turned cold as ice: a great terror and darkness fell upon her; she had never thought that he would ever go away. He caressed her, and played with her as a boy may with a bird before he wrings its neck.

"You will come back?"

He kissed her:—"Surely."

"To-morrow?"

"Nay—not so soon."

"In a week?"

"Hardly."

"In a month, then?"

"Perhaps."

"Before winter, anyway?"

He looked aside from the beseeching, tearful, candid eyes, and kissed her hair and her throat, and said:—"Yes, dear—beyond a doubt."

She clung to him, crying silently—he wished that women would not weep.

"Come, Bébée, listen," he said coaxingly, thinking to break the bitterness to her. "This is not wise, and it gives me pain. There is so much for you to do. You know so little. There is so much to learn. I will leave you many books, and you must grow quite learned in my absence. The Virgin is all very well in her way, but she cannot teach us much, poor lady. For her kingdom is called Ignorance. You must teach yourself. I leave you that to do. The days will go by quickly if you are laborious and patient. Do you love me, little one?"

For an answer she kissed his hand.

"You are a busy little Bébée always," he said, with his lips caressing her soft brown arms that were round his neck. "But you must be busier than ever whilst I am gone. So you will forget. No, no, I do not mean that:—I mean so the time

will pass quickest. And I shall finish your picture,
Bébée, and all Paris will see you, and the great ladies
will envy the little girl with her two wooden shoes.
Ah! that does not please you!—you care for none
of these vanities. No. Poor little Bébée, why did
God make you, or Chance breathe life into you?
You are so far away from us all. It was cruel.
What harm has your poor little soul ever done that,
pure as a flower, it should have been sent to the
hell of this world?"

She clung to him, sobbing without sound. "You
will come back? You will come back?" she moaned,
clasping him closer and closer.

Flamen's own eyes grew dim. But he lied to her:
—"I will—I promise."

It was so much easier to say so, and it would
break her sorrow. So he thought.

For the moment again he was tempted to take
her with him—but, he resisted it—he would tire,
and she would cling to him for ever.

There was long silence. The bleating of the
little kid in the shed without was the only sound;
the grey lavender blew to and fro.

Her arms were close about his throat; he kissed them again, and kissed her eyes, her cheek, her mouth; then put her from him quickly and went out.

She ran to him, and threw herself on the damp ground and held him there, and leaned her forehead on his feet. But though he looked at her with wet eyes, he did not yield, and he still said:—

"I will come back soon—very soon—be quiet, dear, let me go."

Then he kissed her once more many times, and put her gently within the door and closed it.

A low, sharp, sudden cry reached him, went to his heart, but he did not turn; he went on through the wet, green little garden, and the curling leaves, where he had found peace and had left desolation.

## CHAPTER XX.

"I will let her alone and she will marry Jeannot,"
thought Flamen; and he believed himself a good
man for once in his life, and pitied himself for
having become a sentimentalist.

She would marry Jeannot, and bear many
children, as those people always did, and ruddy
little peasants would cling about those pretty, soft,
little breasts of hers; and she would love them after
the manner of such women, and be very content
clattering over the stones in her wooden shoes; and
growing brown and stout, and more careful after
money, and ceasing to dream of unknown things,
and not seeing God at all in the fields, but looking
low and beholding only the ears of the gleaning
wheat and the feet of the tottering children; and so
gaining her bread, and losing her soul, and stooping nearer and nearer to earth till she dropped into
it like one of her own wind-blown wallflowers when

the bee has sucked out all its sweetness and the heats have scorched up all its bloom: — yes, of course, she would marry Jeannot and end so!

Meanwhile he had his Gretchen, and that was the one great matter.

So he left the street of Mary of Burgundy, and went on his way out of the chiming city as its matin bells were rung, and took with him a certain regret, and the only innocent affection that had ever awakened in him; and thought of his self-negation with half admiration and half derision; and so drifted away into the whirlpool of his amorous, cynical, changeful, passionate, callous, many-coloured life, and said to himself as he saw the last line of the low, green plains shine against the sun:—"She will marry Jeannot—of course, she will marry Jeannot. And my Gretchen is greater than Scheffer's."

What else mattered very much after all except what they would say in Paris of Gretchen?

## CHAPTER XXI.

PEOPLE saw that Bébée had grown very quiet. But that was all they saw.

Her little face was pale as she sat amongst her glowing autumn blossoms, by the side of the cobbler's stall, and when the Varnhart children cried at the gate to her to come and play, she would answer gently that she was too busy to have play-time now.

The fruit girl of the Montagne de la Cour hooted after her, "Gone so soon?—ohhè! what did I say? —a fine pine is sugar in the teeth a second only, but the brown nuts you may crack all the seasons round. Well, did you make good harvest while it lasted? has Jeannot a fat bridal portion promised?"

And old Jehan, who was the tenderest soul of them all in the lane by the swans' water, would come and look at her wistfully as she worked amongst the flowers, and would say to her:

"Dear little one, there is some trouble—does it come of that painted picture? You never laugh now, Bébée, and that is bad. A girl's laugh is pretty to hear; my girl laughed like little bells ringing—and then it stopped, all at once; they said she was dead. But you are not dead, Bébée. And yet you are so silent; one would say you were."

But to the mocking of the fruit girl as to the tenderness of old Jehan, Bébée answered nothing; the lines of her pretty curled mouth grew grave and sad, and in her eyes there was a wistful bewildered pathetic appeal like the look in the eyes of a beaten dog, which, while it aches with pain, does not cease to love its master.

One resolve upheld her and made her feet firm on the stones of the streets and her lips mute under all they said to her. She would learn all she could, and be good, and patient, and wise, if trying could make her wise, and so do his will in all things— until he should come back.

"You are not gay, Bébée," said Annémie, who grew so blind that she could scarce see the flags at the mastheads, and who still thought that she pricked

the lace patterns and earned her bread. "You are
not gay, dear. Has any lad gone to sea that your
heart goes away with, and do you watch for his
ship coming in with the coasters? It is weary work
waiting—but it is all the men think us fit for, child.
They may set sail as they like; every new port has
new faces for them; but we are to sit still and to
pray if we like, and never murmur, be the voyage
ever so long, but be ready with a smile and a kiss,
a fresh pipe of tobacco, and a dry pair of socks;—
that is a man. We may have cried our hearts out
—we must have ready the pipe and the socks, or,
'is that what you call love?' they grumble. You
want mortal patience if you love a man,—it is like
a fretful child that thumps you when your breast
is bare to it. Still—be you patient, dear, just as
I am, just as I am."

And Bébée would shudder as she swept the
cobwebs from the garret walls,—patient as she was
—she who had sat here fifty years watching for a
dead man and for a wrecked ship.

## CHAPTER XXII.

THE wheat was reapen in the fields, and the brown earth turned afresh. The white and purple chrysanthemums bloomed against the flowerless rose bushes, and the little grey Michaelmas daisy flourished where the dead carnations had spread their glories. Leaves began to fall, and chilly winds to sigh amongst the willows; the squirrels began to store away their nuts, and the poor to pick up the broken, bare boughs.

"He said he would come before winter," thought Bébée, every day when she rose and felt each morning cooler and greyer than the one before it; winter was near.

Her little feet already were cold in their wooden shoes; and the robin already sang in the twigs of the sear sweetbriar, but she had the brave sweet faith which nothing kills, and she did not doubt—oh! no, she did not doubt, she was only tired.

Tired of the strange, sleepless, feverish nights; tired of the long, dull, empty days; tired of watching down the barren, leafless lane; tired of hearkening breathless to each step on the rustling dead leaves; tired of looking always, always, always, into the ruddy autumn evenings, and the cold autumn star-light, and never hearing what she listened for, never seeing what she sought; tired as a child may be, lost in a wood and wearily wearing its small strength, and breaking its young heart in search of the track for ever missed, of the home for ever beyond the horizon.

Still she did her work and kept her courage.

She took her way into the town with her basket full of the ruby and amber of the dusky autumn blossoms, and when those failed, and the garden was quite desolate, except for a promise of haws and of holly, she went as she had always done, to the lace-room, and gained her bread and the chickens' corn each day by winding the thread round the bobbins; and at nightfall when she had plodded home through the darksome roads, and over the sodden turf, and had lit her rushlight and sat down to her books, with her hand buried in her hair, and her eyes smarting from the strain of the lace-work, and her heart aching with that new and deadly pain which never left her now, she would read—read—read—read, and try and store her brain with knowledge, and try and grasp these vast new meanings of life that the books opened to her, and try and grow less ignorant against he should return.

There was much she could not understand, but there was also much she could.

Her mind was delicate and quick, her intelligence swift and strong; she bought old books at bookstalls with pence that she saved by going without her dinner. The keeper of the stall, a shrewd old soul, explained some hard points to her, and chose good volumes for her, and lent others to this solitary little student in her wooden shoes and with her pale child's face.

So she toiled hard and learned much, and grew taller and very thin, and got a look in her eyes like a lost dog's, and yet never lost heart or wandered in the task that he had set her, or in her faith in his return.

"Burn the books, Bébée," whispered the children again and again, clinging to her skirts. "Burn the wicked, silent things. Since you have had them you never sing, or romp, or laugh, and you look so white—so white."

Bébée kissed them, but kept to her books.

Jeannot going by from the forest night after night saw the light twinkling in the hut window, and sometimes crept softly up and looked through the chinks of the wooden shutter, and saw her leaning over some big old volume with her pretty brows drawn together, and her mouth shut close in earnest effort, and he would curse the man who had changed her so, and go away with rage in his breast and tears in his eyes, not daring to say anything, but knowing that never would Bébée's little brown hand lie in love within his own.

Nor even in friendship, for he had rashly spoken rough words against the stranger from Rubes' Land, and Bébée ever since then had passed him by with a grave simple greeting, and when he had brought her in timid gifts a barrow load of faggots, had thanked him, but had bidden him take the wood home to his mother.

"You think evil things of me, Bébée?" good Jeannot had pleaded, with a sob in his voice; and she had answered gently,—

"No! but do not speak to me, that is all."

Then he had cursed her absent lover, and Bébée had gone within and closed her door.

She had no idea that the people thought ill of her. They were cold to her, and such coldness made her heart ache a little more. But the one great love in her possessed her so strongly that all other things were half unreal.

She did her daily house-work from sheer habit, and she studied because he had told her to do it, and because, with the sweet, stubborn, credulous faith of her youth, she never doubted that he would return.

Otherwise there was no perception of real life in her; she dreamed and prayed, and prayed and dreamed, and never ceased to do either one or the other, even when she was scattering potatoe peels to the fowls, or shaking carrots loose of the soil, or sweeping the snow from her hut door, or going out in the raw dark dawn as the single little sad bell of St. Guido tolled through the stillness for the first mass.

For though even Father Francis looked angered at her because he thought she was stubborn, and hid some truth and some shame from him at confession, yet she went resolutely and oftener than ever to kneel in the dusty, dusky, crumbling old church, for it was all she could do for him, who was absent—so she thought—and she did not feel quite so far away from him when she was beseeching Christ to have care of his soul and of his body.

All her pretty dreams were dead.

She never heard any story in the robin's song, or saw any promise in the sunset clouds, or fancied that angels came about her in the night—never now.

The fields were grey and sad; the birds were little brown things; the stars were cold and far off; the people she had used to care for were like mere shadows that went by her meaningless and without interest, and all she thought of was the one step that never came; all she wanted was the one touch she never felt.

"You have done wrong, Bébée, and you will not own it," said the few neighbours who ever spoke to her.

Bébée looked at them with wistful, uncomprehending eyes.

"I have done no wrong," she said gently, but no one believed her.

A girl did not shut herself up and wane pale and thin for nothing, so they reasoned. She might have sinned as she had liked if she had been sensible after it, and married Jeannot.

But to fret mutely, and shut her lips, and seem as though she had done nothing—that was guilt indeed.

For her village in its small way, thought as the big world thinks.

———

## CHAPTER XXIII.

FULL winter came.

The snow was deep, and the winds drove the people with whips of ice along the dreary country roads and the steep streets of the city. The bells of the dogs and the mules sounded sadly through the white misty silence of the Flemish plains, and the weary horses slipped and fell on the frozen ruts, and on the jagged stones in the little frost-shut Flemish towns. Still the Flemish folk were gay enough in many places.

There were fairs and kermesses; there were puppet-plays and church feasts; there were sledges on the plains and skates on the canals; there were warm woollen hoods and ruddy wood fires; there were tales of demons and saints, and bowls of hot onion soup; sugar images for the little children, and blessed beads for the maidens clasped on rosy throats with lovers' kisses; and in the city itself

there was the high tide of the winter pomp and
mirth, with festal scenes in the churches, and balls
at the palaces, and all manner of gay things in toys
and jewels, and music playing cheerily under the
leafless trees, and flashes of scarlet cloth, and shining furs, and happy faces, and golden curls, in the
carriages that climbed the Montagne de la Cour,
and filled the big place around the statue of stout
Godfrey.

In the little village above St. Guido, Bébée's
neighbours were merry too, in their simple way.

The women worked away wearily at their lace
in the dim winter light, and made a wretched living
by it, but all the same they got penny playthings
for their babies, and a bit of cake for their Sunday
hearth.   They drew together in homely and cordial
friendship, and of an afternoon when dusk fell wove
their lace in company in Mère Kreb's millhouse
kitchen, with the children and the dogs at their feet
on the bricks, so that one big fire might serve for
all, and all be lighted with one big rush candle,
and all be beguiled by chit-chat and songs, stories
of spirits, and whispers of ghosts, and now and

then when the wind howled at its worst, a pater-
noster or two said in common for the men toiling
in the barges or drifting up the Scheldt.

In these gatherings Bébée's face was missed,
and the blithe soft sound of her voice, like a young
thrush singing, was never heard.

The people looked in, and saw her sitting over
a great open book—often her hearth had no fire.

Then the children grew tired of asking her to
play; and their elders began to shake their heads;
she was so pale and so quiet, there must be some
evil in it—so they began to think.

Little by little people dropped away from her.
Who knew, the gossips said, what shame or sin the
child might not have on her sick little soul?

True, Bébée worked hard just the same, and
just the same was seen trudging to and fro in the
dusk of dawns and afternoons in her two little
wooden shoes. She was gentle and laborious, and
gave the children her goat's milk, and the old
women the brambles of her garden.

But they grew afraid of her—afraid of that sad,
changeless, far-away look in her eyes, and of the

mute weariness that was on her—and, being perplexed, were sure, like all ignorant creatures, that
what was secret must be also vile.

So they hung aloof, and let her alone, and by
and by scarcely nodded as they passed her, but
said to Jeannot,—

"You were spared a bad thing, lad; the child
was that grand painter's light-o'-love, that is plain
to see. The mischief all comes of the stuff old
Antoine filled her head with—a stray little bye-
blow of chickweed that he cockered up like a rare
carnation. Oh! do not fly in a rage, Jeannot; the
child is no good, and would have made an honest
man rue. Take heart of grace, and praise the
saints, and marry Katto's Lisa."

But Jeannot would never listen to the slan-
derers, and would never look at Lisa, even though
the door of the little hut was always closed against
him, and whenever he met Bébée on the highway
she never seemed to see him more than she saw
the snow that her sabots were treading.

One night in the midwinter time old Annémie
died.

Bébée found her in the twilight with her head against the garret window, and her left side all shrivelled and useless. She had a little sense left, and a few fleeting breaths to draw.

"Look for the brig," she muttered. "You will not see the flag at the masthead for the fog to-night; but his socks are dry and his pipe is ready. Keep looking—keep looking—she will be in port to-night."

But her dead sailor never came into port; she went to him. The poor, weakened, faithful old body of her was laid in the graveyard of the poor, and the ships came and went under the empty garret window, and Bébée was all alone.

She had no more any thing to work for, or any bond with the lives of others. She could live on the roots of her garden and the sale of her hen's eggs, and she could change the turnips and carrots that grew in a little strip of her ground for the small quantity of bread that she needed.

So she gave herself up to the books, and drew herself more and more within from the outer world. She did not know that the neighbours thought very evil of her; she had only one idea in her mind—to be more worthy of him against he should return.

The winter passed away somehow; she did not know how.

It was a long, cold, white blank of frozen silence; that was all. She studied hard, and had got a quaint, strange, deep scattered knowledge out of her old books; her face had lost all its roundness and colour, but, instead, the forehead had gained breadth, and the eyes had the dim fire of a student's.

Every night when she shut her volumes she thought,—

"I am a little nearer him.    I know a little more."

Just so every morning, when she bathed her hands in the chilly water, she thought to herself, "I will make my skin as soft as I can for him that it may be like the ladies' he has loved."

Love to be perfect must be a religion, as well as a passion.    Bébée's was so.    Like George Herbert's serving maiden, she swept no specks of dirt away from a floor without doing it to the service of her lord.

Only Bébée's lord was a king of earth, made of earth's dust and vanities.

But what did she know of that?

———

## CHAPTER XXIV.

THE winter went by, and the snowdrops and crocus, and pale hepatica smiled at her from the black clods. Every other spring time Bébée had run with fleet feet under the budding trees down into the city, and had sold sweet little wet bunches of violets and briar before all the snow was melted from the eaves of Broodhuis.

"The winter is gone," the townspeople used to say; "look there is Bébée with the flowers."

But this year they did not see the little figure itself like a rosy crocus standing against the brown timbers of the Maison de Roi.

Bébée had not heart to pluck a single blossom of them all. She let them all live, and tended them so that the little garden should look its best and brightest to him when his hand should lift its latch.

Only he was so long coming—so very long—

17*

the violets died away, and the first rosebuds came
in their stead, and still Bébée looked every dawn
and every nightfall vainly down the empty road.

Nothing kills young creatures like the bitterness
of waiting.

Pain they will bear, and privation they will pass
through, fire and water and storm will not appal
them, nor wrath of heaven and earth, but waiting
—the long, tedious, sickly, friendless days, that
drop one by one in their eternal sameness into the
weary past, these kill slowly but surely, as the slow
dropping of water frets away rock.

The summer came.

Nearly a year had gone by. Bébée worked
early and late. The garden bloomed like one big
rose, and the neighbours shook their heads to see
the flowers blossom and fall without bringing in a
single coin.

She herself spoke less seldom than ever, and
now when old Jehan, who never had understood
the evil thoughts of his neighbours, asked her what
ailed her that she looked so pale and never stirred
down to the city, now her courage failed her, and

the tears brimmed over her eyes, and she could not call up a brave brief word, to answer him. For the time was so long, and she was so tired.

Still she never doubted that her lover would come back: he had said he would come: she was as sure that he would come as she was sure that God came in the midst of the people when the silver bell rang and the Host was borne by on high.

Bébée did not heed much, but she vaguely felt the isolation she was left in: as a child too young to reason feels cold and feels hunger.

"No one wants me here now that Annémie is gone," she thought to herself, as the sweet green spring days unfolded themselves one by one like the buds of the briar-rose hedges.

And now and then even the loyal little soul of her gave way, and sobbing on her lonely bed in the long dark nights, she would cry out against him, "Oh, why not have left me alone! I was so happy —so happy!"

And then she would reproach herself with treason to him and ingratitude, and hate herself and feel guilty in her own sight to have thus sinned against him in thought for one single instant.

For there are natures in which the generosity of love is so strong that it feels its own just pain to be disloyalty; and Bébée's was one of them. And if he had killed her she would have died hoping only that no moan had escaped her, under the blow, that ever could accuse him.

These natures, utterly innocent by force of self-accusation and self-abasement, suffer at once the torment of the victim and the criminal.

## CHAPTER XXV.

ONE day in the May weather she sat within doors with a great book upon her table, but no sight for it in her aching eyes. The starling hopped to and fro on the sunny floor; the bees boomed in the porch; the tinkle of sheep's bells came in on the stillness. All was peaceful and happy except the little weary, breaking, desolate heart that beat in her like a caged bird's.

"He will come; I am sure he will come," she said to herself; but she was so tired, and it was so long—oh, dear God!—so very long.

A hand tapped at the lattice. The shrill voice of Reine, the sabot-maker's wife, broken with anguish, called through the hanging ivy,—

"Bébée, you are a wicked one, they say, but the only one there is at home in the village this day. Get you to town for the love of Heaven, and send Doctor Max hither, for my pet, my flower, my child lies dying, and not a soul near, and she black as a coal with choking—go, go, go!—and Mary will forgive you your sins. Save the little one, dear Bébée, do you hear? and I will pray God and speak fair to the neighbours for you. Go!"

Bébée rose up, startled by the now unfamiliar sound of a human voice, and looked at the breathless mother with eyes of pitying wonder.

"Surely I will go," she said, gently; "but there is no need to bribe me. I have not sinned greatly —that I know."

Then she went out quickly and ran through the lanes and into the city for the sick child, and found the wise man, and sent him, and did the errand rather in a sort of sorrowful sympathetic instinct than in any reasoning consciousness of doing good.

When she was moving through the once familiar and happy ways as the sun was setting on the golden fronts of the old houses, and the chimes were ringing from the many towers, a strange sense of unreality, of non-existence fell upon her.

Could it be she?—she indeed—who had gone there the year before the gladdest thing that the earth bore, with no care except to shelter her flowers from the wind, and keep the freshest blossoms for the burgomaster's housewife?

She did not think thus to herself; but a vague doubt that she could ever have been the little gay, laborious, happy Bébée, with troops of friends and endless joys for every day that dawned, came over her as she went by the black front of the Broodhuis.

The strong voice of Lisa, the fruit girl, jarred on her as she passed the stall under its yellow awning that was flapping sullenly in the evening wind.

"Ohhè, little fool," the mocking voice cried, "the rind of the fine pine is full of prickles, and stings the lips when the taste is gone?—to be sure —crack common nuts like me, and you are never wanting—hazels grow free in every copse. Prut, tut! your grand lover lies a-dying; so the students read out of this just now; and you such a simpleton as not to get a roll of napoleons out of him before he went to rot in Paris. I daresay he was poor as sparrows, if one knew the truth. He was only a painter after all."

Lisa tossed her as she spoke a torn sheet, in which she was wrapping gentians: it was a piece of newspaper some three weeks old, and in it there was a single line or so which said that the artist Flamen, whose Gretchen was the wonder of the Salon of the year, lay sick unto death in his rooms in Paris.

Bébée stood and read; the strong ruddy western light upon the type, the taunting laughter of the fruit girl on her ear.

A bitter shriek rang from her that made even the cruelty of Lisa's mirth stop in a sudden terror.

She stood staring like a thing changed to stone down on the one name that to her filled all the universe.

"Ill—he is ill—do you hear?" she echoed piteously, looking at Lisa; "and you say he is poor?"

"Poor? for sure! is he not a painter?" said the fruit girl, roughly. She judged by her own penniless student-lads; and she was angered with herself for feeling sorrow for this little silly thing that she had loved to torture.

"You have been bad and base to me; but now —I bless you, I love you, I will pray for you," said Bébée, in a swift broken breath, and with a look upon her face that startled into pain her callous enemy.

Then without another word, she thrust the paper in her bosom, and ran out of the square breathless with haste and with a great resolve.

He was ill—and he was poor! The brave little soul of her leapt at once to action. He was sick, and far away; and poor, they said. All danger and all difficulty faded to nothing before the vision of his need.

Bébée was only a little foundling who ran about in wooden shoes; but she had the "dog's soul" in her—the soul that will follow faithfully though to receive a curse, that will defend loyally though to meet a blow, and that will die mutely loving to the last.

She went home, how she never knew; and without the delay of a moment packed up a change of linen, and fed the fowls and took the key of the hut down to old Jehan's cabin. The old man was only half-witted by reason of his affliction for his dead daughter, but he was shrewd enough to understand what she wanted of him, and honest enough to do it.

"I am going into the city," she said to him; "and if I am not back to-night, will you feed the starling and the hens, and water the flowers for me?"

Old Jehan put his head out of his lattice; it was seven in the evening, and he was going to bed.

"What are you after, little one?" he asked; "going to show the fine buckles at a students' ball? Nay, fie—that is not like you."

"I am going to—pray,—dear Jehan," she answered, with a sob in her throat and the first falsehood she ever had told. "Do what I ask you—do for your dead daughter's sake—or the birds and the flowers will die of hunger and thirst. Take the key and promise me."

He took the key and promised.

"Do not let them see those buckles shine; they will rob you," he added.

Bébée ran from him fast; every moment that was lost was so precious and so terrible. To pause a second for fear's sake never occurred to her. She went forth as fearlessly as a young swallow, born in northern April days, flies forth on instinct to new lands and over unknown seas when autumn falls.

Necessity and action breathed new life into her. The hardy and brave peasant ways of her were awoke once more. She had been strong to wait silently with the young life in her dying out drop by drop in the heartsickness of long delay. She was strong now to throw herself into strange countries and dim perils and immeasurable miseries, on the sole chance that she might be of service to him.

A few human souls here and there can love like dogs. Bébée's was one.

## CHAPTER XXVI.

IT was dark. The May days are short in the north lands of the Scheldt.

She had her little winter cloak of frieze and her wooden shoes and her little white cap, with the sunny curls rippling out of it in their pretty rebellion. She had her little lanthorn too; and her bundle; and she had put a few fresh eggs in her basket, with some sweet herbs and the palm-sheaf that Father Francis had blessed last Easter—for who could tell, she thought, how ill he might not be, or how poor?

She hardly gave a look to the hut as she ran by its garden gate; all her heart was on in front, in the vague far-off country where he lay sick unto death.

She ran fast through the familiar lanes into the city. She was not very sure where Paris was, but she had the name clear and firm, and she knew that people were always coming and going thence and thither, so that she had no fear she should not find it.

She went straight to the big busy bewildering place in the Leopold quarter where the iron horses fumed every day and night along the iron ways. She had never been there before, but she knew it was by that great highway that the traffic to Paris was carried on, and she knew that it would carry people also as well.

There were bells clanging, lights flashing, and crowds pushing and shouting, as she ran up—a little grey figure, with the lantern spark glimmering like any tiny glow-worm astray in a gaslit city.

"To Paris?" she asked, entreatingly, going where she saw others going, to a little grated wicket in a wall.

"Twenty-seven francs—quick!" they demanded of her.

Bébée gave a great cry, and stood still, trembling and trying not to sob aloud. She had never thought of money; she had forgotten that youth and strength and love and willing feet and piteous prayers—all went for nothing as this world is made.

A hope flashed on her, and a glad thought. She loosed the silver buckles, and held them out.

"Would you take these? They are worth much more."

There was a derisive laughter; some one bade her with an oath begone; rough shoulders jostled her away. She stretched her arms out piteously.

"Take me—oh, pray take me! I will go with the sheep, with the cattle—only, only, take me!"

But in the rush and roar none heeded her; some thief snatched the silver buckles from her hand, and made off with them and was lost in the throng; a great iron beast rushed by her, snorting flame and bellowing smoke; there was a roll like thunder, and all was dark: the night express had passed on its way to Paris.

Bébée stood still, crushed for a moment with the noise and the cruelty and the sense of absolute desolation; she scarcely noticed that the buckles had been stolen; she had only one thought—to get to Paris.

"Can I never go without money?" she asked at the wicket; the man there glanced a moment, with a touch of pity, at the little wistful face.

"The least is twenty francs—surely you must know that?" he said, and shut his grating with a clang.

Bébée turned away and went out of the great cruel tumultuous place; her heart ached and her brain was giddy, but the sturdy courage of her nature rose to need.

"There is no way at all to go without money to Paris, I suppose?" she asked of an old woman whom she knew a little, who sold nuts and little pictures of saints and wooden playthings under the trees, in the avenue hard by.

The old woman shook her head.

"Eh?—no, dear. There is nothing to be done anywhere in the world without money. Look, I cannot get a litre of nuts to sell unless I pay beforehand."

"Would it be far to walk?"

"Far! Holy Jesus! It is right away in the heart of France—over two hundred miles, they say; straight out through the forest. Not but what my son did walk it once—and he a shoemaker, who knows what walking costs; and he is well to do there now—not that he ever writes. When they want nothing people never write."

"And he walked into Paris?"

"Yes, ten years ago. He had nothing but a few sous and an ash stick, and he had a fancy to try his luck there. And after all our feet were given us to travel with. If you go there and you see him, tell him to send me something—I am tired of selling nuts."

Bébée said nothing, but went on her road; since there was no other way but to walk she would take that way; the distance and the hardship did not appal two little feet that were used to traverse so many miles of sun-baked summer dust and of frozen winter mud unblenchingly year after year.

The time it would take made her heart sink indeed. He was ill. God knew what might happen. But neither the length of leagues nor the fatigue of body daunted her. She only saw his eyes dim with pain and his lips burned with fever.

She would walk twenty miles a day, and then, perhaps, she might get lifts here and there on hay waggons or in pedlars' carts; people had always used to be kind to her. Anyhow she counted she might reach Paris well in fifteen days.

She sat under a shrine in a bye street a moment, and counted the copper pieces she had on her; they were few, and the poor pretty buckles that she might have sold to get money, were stolen.

She had some twenty sous and a dozen eggs; she thought she might live on that; she had wanted to take the eggs to him, but after all, to keep life in her until she could reach Paris was the one great thing.

"What a blessing it is to have been born poor; and to have lived hardly—one wants so little!" she thought to herself.

Then she put up the sous in the linen bosom of her gown, and trimmed her little lantern and knelt down in the quiet darkness and prayed a moment, with the hot agonised tears rolling down her face, and then rose and stepped out bravely in the cool of the night, on the great south-west road towards Paris.

The thought never once crossed her to turn
back, and go again into the shelter of her own little
hut among the flowers.  He was sick there, dying,
for anything she knew—that was the only thing she
remembered.

It was a clear, starlit night, and everywhere the
fragrance of the spring was borne in from the wide
green plains, and the streams where the rushes were
blowing.

She walked ten miles easily, the beautiful
grey shadow all about her.  She had never been
so far from home in all her life, except to
that one Kermesse at Mechlin.  But she was not
afraid.

With the movement, and the air, and the sense
that she was going to him, which made her happy
even in her misery, something of the old, sweet,
lost fancies came to her.

She smiled at the stars through her tears, and
as the poplars swayed and murmured in the wind,
they looked to her like the wings and the swords
of a host of angels.

Her way lay out through the forest, and in that

sweet green woodland, she was not afraid—no more afraid than the fawns were.

At Boitsfort she shrank a little, indeed. Here there were the open-air restaurants, and the café gardens all alight for the pleasure-seekers from the city; here there were music and laughter, and horses with brass bells, and bright colours on high in the wooden balconies, and below among the blossoming hawthorn hedges. She had to go through it all, and she shuddered a little as she ran, thinking of that one priceless, deathless, forest day when he had kissed her first.

But the pleasure-people were all busied with their mirth and mischief, and took no notice of the little grey figure in the starry night. She went on along the grassy roads, under the high arching trees, with the hoot of the owls and the cry of the rabbits on the stillness.

At Groenendael, in the heart of the forest, midnight was striking as she entered the village. Everyone was asleep. The lights were all out. The old ruined priory frowned dark under the clouds.

She shivered a little again, and began to feel

chill and tired, yet did not dare to knock at any one of the closed house-doors—she had no money.

So she walked on her first ten unknown miles, meeting a few people only, and being altogether unmolested—a small grey figure, trotting in two little wooden shoes.

They thought her a peasant going to a fair or a lace mill, and no one did her more harm than to wish her good-night in rough Flemish.

When the dawn began to whiten above the plains of the east, she saw an empty cowshed filled with hay; she was a little tired, and lay down and rested an hour or two, as a young lamb might have lain on the dried clover, for she knew that she must keep her strength and husband her power, or never reach across the dreary length of the foreign land to Paris.

But by full sunrise she was on her way again, bathing her face in a brook and buying a sou's worth of bread and flet milk at the first cottage that she passed in bright, leaf-bowered Hoeylaert.

The forest was still all around her, with its exquisite life of bough and blossom, and murmur of insect and of bird. She told her beads, praying as she went, and was almost happy.

God would not let him die. Oh no, not till she had kissed him once more, and could die with him.

The hares ran across the path, and the blue butterflies flew above head. There was purple gloom of pinewood, and sparkling verdure of aspen and elm. There were distant church carillons ringing, and straight golden shafts of sunshine streaming.

She was quite sure God would not let him die.

She hoped that he might be very poor. At times he had talked as if he were, and then she might be of so much use. She knew how to deal with fever and suffering. She had sat up many a night with the children of the village. The grey sisters had taught her many of their ways of battling with disease; and she could make fresh cool drinks, and she could brew beautiful remedies from simple herbs. There was so much that she might do; her fancy played with it almost happily. And then, only to touch his hand, only to hear his voice; her heart rose at the thought, as a lark to its morning song.

At Rixensart, buried in its greenery, as she went through it in morning light, some peasants greeted her cheerily, and called to her to rest in a house-porch, and gave her honey and bread. She could not eat much; her tongue was parched and her throat was dry, but the kindness was precious to her, and she went on her road the stronger for it.

"It is a long way to walk to Paris," said the woman, with some curious wonder. Bébée smiled, though her eyes grew wet.

"She has the look of the little Gesù," said the Rixensart people, and they watched her away with a vague timid pity.

So she went on through Ottignies and La Roche, to Villers, and left the great woods and the city chimes behind her, and came through the green abbey valleys through Tilly and Ligny, and

Fleurus, and so into the coal and iron fields that lie round Charleroi.

Here her heart grew sick, and her courage sank under the noise and the haste, before the blackness and the hideousness. She had never seen anything like it. She thought it was hell, with the naked, swearing, fighting people, and the red fires leaping night and day. Nevertheless, if hell it were, since it lay betwixt her and him, she found force to brave and cross it.

The miners and glass-blowers and nail-makers, rough and fierce and hard, frightened her. The women did not look like women, and the children ran and yelled at her, and set their dogs upon her. The soil was thick with dust like soot, and the trees were seared and brown. There was no peace in the place, and no loveliness. Eighty thousand folks toiled together in the hopeless Tophet, and swarmed, and struggled, and laboured, and multiplied, in joyless and endless wrestling against hunger and death.

She got through it somehow, hiding often from the ferocious youngsters, and going sleepless rather than lie in those dens of filth; but she seemed so many, many years older when Charleroi lay at last behind her—so many, many years older than when she had sat and spun in the garden at home.

When she was once in the valley of the Sambre she was more herself again, only she felt weaker than she had ever done, because she only dared to spend one of her sous each day, and one sou got so little food.

In the woods and fields about Alne she began to breathe again, like a bird loosed to the air after being shut in a wooden trap. Green corn, green boughs, green turf, mellow chimes of church bells, humming of golden bees, cradle songs of women spinning, homely odours of little herb gardens and of orchard trees under cottage walls—these had been around her all her life; she only breathed freely amongst them.

She often felt tired, and her wooden shoes were wearing so thin that the hot dust of the road at noonday burnt her feet through them. Sometimes, too, she felt a curious brief faintness such as she had never known, for the lack of food and the long fatigue began to tell even on her hardy little body. But she went on bravely, rarely doing less than her twenty miles a day, and sometimes more, walking often in the night to save time, and lying down in cowsheds or under haystacks in the noontide.

For the most part people were kind to her; they saw she was so very young and so poor.

Women would give her leave to bathe herself in their bed-chambers, and children would ask her to wait on the village bench under the chestnut tree, while they brought her their pet lamb or their tumbler pigeons to look at, but, for the most part —unless she was very, very tired—she would not wait. It took her so long, and who could tell how it fared with him in Paris?

Into the little churches, scattered over the wide countries between Charleroi and Erquelinnes, she would turn aside, indeed; but, then, that was only to say a prayer for him; that was not loss to him, but gain.

So she walked on until she reached the frontier

of France. She began to get a little giddy; she began to see the blue sky and the green level always swirling round her as if some one were spinning them to frighten her, but still she would not be afraid; she went on, and on, and on, till she set her last step on the soil of Flanders.

Here a new strange, terrible, incomprehensible obstacle opposed her: she had no papers; they thrust her back and spoke to her as if she were a criminal. She could not understand what they could mean. She had never heard of these laws and rules. She vaguely comprehended that she must not enter France, and stunned and heartbroken she dropped down under a tree, and for the first time sobbed as if her very life would weep itself away.

She could see nothing, understand nothing. There were the same road, the same hedges, the same fields, the same white cottages, and peasants in blue shirts and dunhued oxen in the waggons. She saw no mark, no difference, ere they told her where she stood was Belgium, and where they stood was France, and that she must not pass from one into the other.

The men took no notice of her. They went back into their guardhouse, and smoked and drank. A cat sunned herself under a scarlet bean. The white clouds sailed on before a southerly sky. She might die here—he there—and nothing seemed to care.

After a while an old hawker came up; he was travelling with wooden clocks from the Black Forest. He stopped and looked at her, and asked her what she ailed.

She knelt down at his feet in the dust.

"Oh, help me!" she cried to him. "Oh, pray, help me! I have walked all the way from Brussels —that is my country, and now they will not let me pass that house where the soldiers are. They say I have no papers. What papers should I have? I do not know. When one has done no harm, and does not owe a sou anywhere, and has walked all the way—Is it money that they want? I have none; and they stole my silver clasps in Brussels;

and if I do not get to Paris I must die—die without seeing him again—ever again, dear God!"

She dropped her head upon the dust and crouched and sobbed there, her courage broken by this new barrier that she had never dreamed would come between herself and Paris.

The old hawker looked at her thoughtfully. He had seen much of men and women, and knew truth from counterfeit, and he was moved by the child's agony.

He stooped and whispered in her ear.

"Get up quick, and I will pass you. It is against the law, and I may go to prison for it. Never mind; one must risk something in this world, or else be a cur. My daughter has stayed behind in Marbais sweethearting; her name is on my passport, and her age and face will do for yours. Get up and follow me close, and I will get you through. Poor little soul, whatever your woe is it is real enough, and you are such a young and pretty thing. Get up, the guards are in their house, they have not seen; follow me, and you must not speak a word; they must take you for a German, dumb as wood."

She got up and obeyed him, not comprehending, but only vaguely seeing that he was friendly to her, and would pass her over into France.

The old man made a little comedy at the barrier, and scolded her as though she were his daughter for losing her way as she came to meet him, and then crying like a baby.

The guards looked at her carelessly, joked the hawker on her pretty face, looked the papers over, and let her through, believing her the child of the clock-maker of the Hartz. Some lies are blessed as truth.

"I have done wrong in the law, but not before God, I think, little one," said the pedlar. "Nay —do not thank me, or go on like that; we are in sight of the Customs men still, and if they suspected, it would be the four walls of a cell only that you and I should see to-night. And now tell me your story, poor maiden—why are you on foot through a strange country?"

But Bébée would not tell him her story; she

was confused and dazed still. She did not know rightly what had happened to her; but she could not talk of herself, nor of why she travelled thus to Paris.

The old hawker got cross at her silence, and called her an unthankful jade, and wished that he had left her to her fate, and parted company with her at two cross-roads, saying his path did not lie with hers; and then when he had done that, was sorry, and being a tender-hearted soul, hobbled back, and would fain press a five-franc piece on her; and Bébée, refusing it all the while, kissed his old brown hands and blessed him, and broke away from him, and so went on again solitary towards St. Quentin.

The country was very flat and poor, and yet the plains had a likeness in them to her own wide Brabant downs, where the tall green wheat was blowing and the barges dropping down the sluggish streams.

She was very footsore; very weary; very hungry so often; but she was in France—in his country;—

and her spirit rose with the sense of that nearness to him.

After all God was so good to her; there were fine bright days and nights; a few showers had fallen, but merely passing ones; the air was so cool and so balmy that it served her almost as food; and she seldom found people so unkind that they refused for her single little sou to give her a crust of bread and let her lie in an outhouse.

After all God was very good; and by the sixteenth or seventeenth day she would be in the city of Paris.

She was a little lightheaded at times from insufficient nourishment; especially after waking from strange dreams in unfamiliar places; sometimes the soil felt tremulous under her, and the sky spun round; but she struggled against the feeling, and kept a brave heart, and tried to be afraid of nothing.

Sometimes at night she thought she saw old Annémie. "But what if I do?" she said to herself; "Annémie never will hurt me."

And now, as she grew nearer her goal, her natural buoyancy of spirit returned as it had never done to her since the evening that he had kissed and left her. As her body grew lighter and more exhausted, her fancy grew keener and more dominant. All things of the earth and air spoke to her as she went along as they had used to do. All that she had learned from the books in the long cold months came to her clear and wonderful. She was not so very ignorant now—ignorant, indeed, beside him—but still knowing something that would make her able to read to him if he liked it, and to understand if he talked of grave things.

She had no fixed thought of what she would be to him when she reached him.

She fancied she would wait on him, and tend him, and make him well, and be caressed by him, and get all gracious pretty things of leaf and blossom about him, and kneel at his feet, and be quite happy if he only touched her now and then with his lips;—her thoughts went no farther than that;—her love for him was of that intensity and absorption in which nothing but itself is remembered.

When a creature loves much, even when it is as little and as simple a soul as Bébée, the world and all its people and all its laws and ways are as nought. They cease to exist; they are as though they had never been.

Whoever recollects an outside world may play with passion, or may idle with sentiment, but does not love.

She did not hear what the villagers said to her. She did not see the streets of the towns as she passed them. She kept herself clean always, and broke fast now and then by sheer instinct of habit, nothing more. She had no perception what she did, except of walking—walking—walking always, and seeing the white road go by like pale ribbons unrolled.

She got a dreamy, intense, sleepless light in her blue eyes that frightened some of those she passed. They thought she had been fever-stricken, and was not in her senses.

So she went across the dreary lowlands, wearing
out her little sabots, but not wearing out her patience and her courage.

She was very dusty and jaded. Her woollen
skirt was stained with weather and torn with briars.
But she had managed always to wash her cap
white in brook-water, and she had managed always
to keep her pretty bright curls soft and silken—for
he had liked them so much, and he would soon
draw them through his hand again. So she told
herself a thousand times to give her strength when
the mist would come over her sight, and the earth
would seem to tremble as she went. On the fifteenth
day from the night when she had left her hut by
the swans' water, Bébée saw Paris.

Shining away in the sun; white and gold;
amongst woods and gardens she saw Paris.

She was so tired—oh, so tired—but she could
not rest now. There were bells ringing always in
her ears, and a heavy pain always in her head. But
what of that?—she was so near to him.

"Are you ill, you little thing?" a woman asked

her who was gathering early cherries in the outskirts of the great city.

Bébée looked at her and smiled: "I do not know —I am happy."

And she went onward.

It was evening. The sun had set. She had not eaten for twenty-four hours. But she could not pause for anything now. She crossed the gleaming river, and she heard the cathedral chimes. Paris in all its glory was about her, but she took no more note of it than a pigeon that flies through it intent on reaching home.

No one looked at or stopped her; a little dusty peasant with a bundle on a stick over her shoulder.

The click clack of her wooden shoes on the hot pavements made none look up; little rustics came up every day like this to make their fortunes in Paris. Some grew into golden painted silken flowers, the convolvuli of their brief summer days; and some drifted into the Seine water, rusted, wind-tossed, fallen leaves, that were wanted of no man. Anyhow it was so common to see them, pretty but homely things, with their noisy shoes and their little all in a bundle, that no one even looked once at Bébée.

She was not bewildered. As she had gone through her own city, only thinking of the roses in her basket, and of old Annémie in her garret, so she went through Paris, only thinking of him for whose sake she had come thither.

Now that she was really in his home she was happy; happy though her head ached with that dull odd pain, and all the sunny glare went round and round like a great gilded humming-top, such as the babies clapped their hands at at Kermesse.

She was happy; she felt sure now that God would not let him die till she got to him. She was quite glad that he had left her all that long, terrible winter, for she had learned so much and was so much more fitted to be with him.

Weary as she was, and strange as the pain in her head made her feel, she was happy, very happy; a warm flush came on her little pale cheeks as she thought how soon he would kiss them, her whole body thrilled with the old sweet nameless joy that she had sickened for in vain so long.

Though she saw no thing else that was around her, she saw some little knots of moss roses that a girl was selling on the quay, as she used to sell them in front of the Maison du Roi. She had only two sous left, but she stopped and bought two little rosebuds to take to him. He had used to care for them so much in the summer in Brabant.

The girl who sold them told her the way to the street he lived in; it was not very far off the quay. She seemed to float on air, to have wings like the swallows, to hear beautiful music all around. She felt for her beads, and said aves of praise. God was so good.

It was quite night when she reached the street, and sought the number of his house. She spoke his name softly, and trembling very much with joy, not with any fear, but it seemed to her too sacred a thing ever to utter aloud.

An old man looked out of a den by the door, and told her to go straight up the stairs to the

third floor, and then turn to the right. The old
man chuckled as he glanced after her, and listened
to the wooden shoes pattering wearily up the broad
stone steps.

Bébée climbed them—ten, twenty, thirty, forty.
"He must be very poor!" she thought, "to live so
high," and yet the place was wide and handsome,
and had a look of riches. Her heart beat so fast,
she felt suffocated; her limbs shook, her eyes had
a red blood-like mist floating before them; but she
thanked God each step she climbed—a moment,
and she would look upon the only face she loved.

"He will be glad;—oh, I am sure he will be
glad!" she said to herself, as a fear that had never
before come near her touched her for a moment—
if he should not care?

But even then, what did it matter? Since he
was ill she should be there to watch him night and
day, and when he was well again, if he should wish
her to go away—one could always die.

"But he will be glad—oh, I know he will be
glad," she said to the rose-buds that she carried to

him. "And if God will only let me save his life, what else do I want more?"

His name was written on a door before her. The handle of a bell hung down, she pulled it timidly. The door unclosed, she saw no one, and went through. There were low lights burning. There were heavy scents that were strange to her. There was a fantastic gloom from old armour, and old weapons, and old pictures in the dull rich chambers. The sound of her wooden shoes was lost in the softness and thickness of the carpets.

It was not the home of a poor man. A great terror froze her heart;—if she were not wanted here?

She went quickly through three rooms, seeing no one, and at the end of the third there were folding doors.

"It is I—Bébée," she said softly, as she pushed them gently apart; and she held out the two moss rosebuds.

Then the words died on her lips, and a great horror froze her, still and silent, there.

She saw the dusky room as in a dream. She

saw him stretched on the bed, leaning on his elbow, laughing, and playing cards upon the lace coverlet. She saw women with loose shining hair and bare limbs, and rubies and diamonds glimmering red and white. She saw men lying about upon the couch, throwing dice and drinking and laughing one with another.

Beyond all she saw against the pillows of his bed a beautiful brown wicked-looking thing like some velvet snake who leaned over him as he threw down the painted cards upon the lace, and who had cast about his throat her curved bare arm with the great coils of dead gold all a-glitter on it.

And above it all there were odours of wines and flowers, clouds of smoke, shouts of laughter, music of shrill gay voices.

She stood like a frozen creature and saw—the rosebuds in her hand. Then with a great piercing cry she let the little roses fall, and turned and fled. At the sound he looked up and saw her, and shook his beautiful brown harlot off him with an oath.

But Bébée flew down through the empty chambers and the long stairway as a hare flies from the hounds; her tired feet never paused, her aching limbs never slackened; she ran on, and on, and on, into the lighted streets, into the fresh night air; on, and on, and on, straight to the river.

From its brink some man's strength caught and held her. She struggled with it.

"Let me die, let me die!" she shrieked to him and strained from him to get at the cool grey silent water that waited for her there.

Then she lost all consciousness, and saw the stars no more.

When she came back to any sense of life, the stars were shining still, and the face of Jeannot was bending over her, wet with tears.

He had followed her to Paris when they had missed her first, and had come straight by train to the city, making sure it was thither she had come, and there had sought her many days, watching for her by the house of Flamen.

She shuddered away from him as he held her, and looked at him with blank tearless eyes.

"Do not touch me—take me home."

That was all she ever said to him. She never asked him or told him anything. She never noticed that it was strange that he should have been here upon the river bank. He let her be, and took her silently in the cool night back by the iron ways to Brabant.

———

## CHAPTER XXVII.

SHE sat quite still and upright in the waggon, with the dark lands rushing by her. She never spoke at all. She had a look that frightened him upon her face. When he tried to touch her hand, she shivered away from him.

The charcoal-burner, hardy and strong amongst forest-reared men, cowered like a child in a corner, and covered his eyes and wept.

So the night wore away.

She had no perception of anything that happened to her until she was led through her own little garden in the early day, and her starling cried to her "Bonjour, Bonjour!" Even then she only looked about her in a bewildered way, and never spoke.

Were the sixteen days a dream!

She did not know.

The women whom Jeannot summoned, his
mother and sisters, and Mère Krebs, and one or
two others, weeping for what had been the hard-
ness of their hearts against her, undressed her, and
laid her down on her little bed, and opened the
shutters to the radiance of the sun.

She let them do as they liked, only she seemed
neither to hear nor see, and she never spoke.

All that Jeannot could tell was that he had
found her in Paris, and had saved her from the
river.

The women were sorrowful, and reproached
themselves. Perhaps she had done wrong, but they
had been harsh, and she was so young.

The two little sabots with the holes worn
through the soles touched them; and they blamed
themselves for having shut their hearts and their
doors against her as they saw the fixed blue eyes,
without any light in them, and the pretty mouth
closed close against either sob or smile.

After all she was Bébée—the little bright blithe
thing that had danced with their children, and sung
to their singing, and brought them always the first

roses of the year.   If she had been led astray, they
should have been gentler with her.

So they told themselves and each other.

What had she seen in that terrible Paris to
change her like this?—they could not tell.   She
never spoke.

The cock crowed gaily to the sun.   The lamb
bleated in the meadow.   The bees boomed amongst
the pear-tree blossoms.   The grey lavender blew in
the open house-door.   The green leaves threw shifting shadows on the floor.

All things were just the same as they had been
the year before, when she had woke to the joy of
being a girl of sixteen.

But Bébée now lay quite still and silent on her
little bed; as quiet as the waxen Gesù that they
laid in the manger at the Nativity.

"If she would only speak!" the women and the
children wailed, weeping sorely.

But she never spoke; nor did she seem to know
any one of them.   Not even the starling, as he flew
on her pillow and called her.

"Give her rest," they all said; and one by one moved away, being poor folk and hard-working, and unable to lose a whole day.

Mère Krebs stayed with her, and Jeannot sat in the porch where her little spinning wheel stood, and rocked himself to and fro; in vain agony, powerless.

He had done all he could, and it was of no avail.

Then people who had loved her, hearing, came up the green lanes from the city—the cobbler and the tinman, and the old woman who sold saints' pictures by the Broodhuis. The Varnhart children hung about the garden wicket, frightened and sobbing. Old Jehan beat his knees with his hands, and said only, over and over again, "Another dead —another dead!—the red mill and I see them all dead."

The long golden day drifted away, and the swans swayed to and fro, and the willows grew silver in the sunshine.

Bébée, only, lay quite still and never spoke.

The starling sat above her head; his wings drooped, and he was silent too.

Towards sunset Bébée raised herself and called aloud: they ran to her.

"Get me a rosebud—one with the moss round it," she said to them.

They went out into the garden, and brought her one wet with dew.

She kissed it, and laid it in one of her little wooden shoes that stood upon the bed.

"Send them to him," she said wearily; "tell him I walked all the way."

Then her head drooped; then momentary consciousness died out: the old dull, lifeless look crept over her face again like the shadow of death.

The starling spread his broad black wings above her head. She lay quite still once more. The women left the rosebud in the wooden shoes, not knowing what she meant.

Night fell. Mère Krebs watched beside her. Jeannot went down to the old church to beseech heaven with all his simple, ignorant, tortured soul. The villagers hovered about, talking in low sad voices, and wondering, and dropping one by one into their homes. They were sorry, very sorry; but what could they do?

It was quite night. The lights were put out in the lane. Jeannot, with Father Francis, prayed before the shrine of the Seven Sorrows. Mère Krebs slumbered in her rush-bottomed chair; she was old and worked hard. The starling was awake.

Bébée rose in her bed, and looked around, as she had done when she had asked for the moss rosebud.

A sense of unutterable universal pain ached over all her body.

She did not see her little home, its four white walls, its lattice shining in the moon, its wooden bowls and plates, its oaken shelf and presses, its plain familiar things that once had been so dear: —she did not see them;—she only saw the brown woman with her arm about his throat.

She sat up in her bed and slipped her feet on

to the ground; the pretty little rosy feet that he had used to want to clothe in silken stockings.

Poor little feet! she felt a curious compassion for them;—they had served her so well, and they were so tired.

She sat up a moment with that curious dull agony, aching everywhere in body and in brain. She kissed the rosebud once more, and laid it gently down in the wooden shoe. She did not see anything that was around her. She felt a great dulness that closed in on her; a great weight that was like iron on her head.

She thought she was in the strange, noisy, cruel city, with the river close to her, and all her dead dreams drifting down it like murdered children, whilst that woman kissed him.

She slipped her feet on to the floor, and rose and stood upright. There was a door open to the moonlight—the door where she had sat spinning and singing in a thousand happy days; the lavender blew; the tall, unbudded green lilies swayed in the

20*

wind; she looked at them, and knew none of them.

The night air drifted through her linen dress, and played on her bare arms, and lifted the curls of her hair; the same air that had played with her so many times out of mind when she had been a little tottering thing that measured its height by the red rosebush. But it brought her no sense of where she was.

All she saw was the woman who kissed him.

There was the water beyond; the kindly calm water, all green with the moss and the nests of the ouzels and the boughs of the hazels and willows, where the swans were asleep in the reeds, and the broad lilies spread wide and cool.

But she did not see any memory in it. She thought it was the cruel grey river in the strange white city; and she cried to it; and went out into the old familiar ways, and knew none of them; and ran feebly yet fleetly through the bushes and flowers, looking up once at the stars with a helpless broken blind look, like a thing that is dying.

"He does not want me!" she said to them.
"He does not want me!—other women kiss him
there!"

Then with a low fluttering sound like a bird's
when its wings are shot, and yet it tries to rise, she
hovered a moment over the water, and stretched
her arms out to it.

"He does not want me!" she murmured; "he
does not want me—and I am so tired. Dear
God!"

Then she crept down, as a weary child creeps
to its mother, and threw herself forward, and let
the green dark waters take her where they had
found her amidst the lilies, a little laughing yearling
thing.

There she soon lay, quite quiet, with her face
turned to the stars, and the starling poised above to
watch her as she slept.

She had been only Bébée—the ways of God and
man had been too hard for her.

When the messengers of Flamen came that day,
they took him back a dead moss-rose and a

pair of little wooden shoes worn through with walking.

"One creature loved me once," he says to women who wonder why the wooden shoes are there.

THE END.

www.ingramcontent.com/pod-product-compliance
Lightning Source LLC
Chambersburg PA
CBHW031401270326
41929CB00010BA/1283